# BEYOND GENDER AND
# ETHNIC STEREOTYPES

# BEYOND GENDER AND ETHNIC STEREOTYPES

## HOW WOMEN OF COLOR REDEFINE PUBLIC SECTOR LEADERSHIP

Angela R. McCullough

MANUSCRIPTS
PRESS

BEYOND GENDER AND ETHNIC STEREOTYPES
*How Women of Color Redefine Public Sector Leadership*

ISBN     979-8-88926-871-0  *Paperback*
         979-8-88926-872-7  *Hardcover*
         979-8-88926-870-3  *Ebook*

# CONTENTS

——

# AUTHOR'S NOTE

———

As I began my journey to write this book, my initial goal was to amplify the voices of women of color, which is a critical and necessary task. However, as I progressed midway through the process, I experienced a sudden awakening of my spirit, which left me unable to proceed further. At that time, I didn't fully understand the reason behind this feeling.

I believe amplifying the voices of Black women is crucial and necessary work. For this reason, I have focused on centering this book in the public sector, where our voices are often missing from important policy decisions. As a Black woman, I envision that more of us will enter public sector spaces and have fulfilling careers leading us to executive positions. This way, we can contribute to creating policies informed by our lived experiences. Our communities face numerous challenges, such as food deserts, homelessness, mental health, joblessness, and inadequate education. We are in crisis and require critical voices from people in power who look like us to help reshape policies.

I did not intend to place the book at the center of the diversity, equity, and inclusion (DEI) space. To me, it is just a collection of words and letters frequently used. In my experience, using these words at the workplace is often only performative. After the George Floyd murder, there was a surge of energy around changing the system, but without any real work and money to tear down the structures still haunting us in this country. I have realized we should focus on more than just DEI by creating spaces where we all belong. We need places where we feel welcome, heard, respected, and valued. We need to know that our opinions matter and that people are willing to listen and change course based on what we say.

The women in the following chapters lend their voices as a guide in helping other women reach their career goals. Their stories celebrate overcoming the often-insurmountable challenges of living and working within a white supremacist society. The system and the structures flash a neon light, reminding you that it is closed to women of color.

The time is now to counter that narrative. Understanding that progress means perseverance plus influential sponsorship is the key to executive leadership in the public sector for women of color.

As a fifty-three-year-old, having been the first in many instances, I want to make sure I share my experience and what I've learned over my career to open the door for others. We are all unique and should have the same opportunities. I hope to encourage women considering career options or already in the workforce to join the space to move toward a future where being the first is no longer a thing and diversity, inclusion, and belonging are the norm.

With gratitude,
Angela

# INTRODUCTION

———

"They only hired you to comply with affirmative action," a colleague said to me in a quiet whisper within the first few months of my new public sector job.

I stood there frozen, looking directly at him as my heart beat faster. Thoughts quickly flooded my mind. Am I safe? Do I have to be concerned about working in the building alone? Who would help me if something happened? How would my parents find out if I was hurt or missing?

I remember the phone call from my mother that started me on my career path. She said, "There's a letter here for you from the federal government."

In a rather high-pitched voice, I responded, "Really? Please open it."

I heard the sound of tearing paper as my mother opened the envelope. I had no idea what to expect. Reading from the letter, my mother said, "We would like to invite you to apply for a position in our agency. We see that you have recently left the Air Force, and we believe your skills will be transferrable to our work."

I was surprised, so I quickly phoned the contact in the letter and then applied for a position. Within a few months, I started my career as a public servant working for the federal government in Evansville, Indiana. Having grown up in Detroit, Michigan, Evansville was a bit of a culture shock with its small-town vibe.

I entered my new job as an early twenty-something filled with the joy of new opportunities and the hope of a fulfilling career. A staff of white men, all as old as my father and grandfather, greeted me. I was alone. There were no other female electronics technicians or no other people of color. One coworker and his wife welcomed me and helped me settle into the area, sharing valuable local information to help me transition. Everyone else was not quite as welcoming. Within the first few months of employment, one of my new coworkers let me know that because of my gender and race, I wasn't wanted.

After my initial fear from my colleague's whisper had subsided, I took deep breaths to still myself and focus my thoughts. I would be just fine. It was his way of letting me know that I didn't deserve or that I was not qualified to be there. I had only walked through those doors because I was a Black woman—nothing more than a number, a part of a quota system. He had a lot of audacity, I thought. I had served this country and defended the Constitution, and I had earned my ticket into the coveted federal halls.

With quiet determination, I turned and walked away. I knew he and the other men I worked with had knowledge and experience that I didn't have, and I needed to develop. I instantly vowed to myself that I would learn all I could from them and would gain their respect by working hard and accomplishing my work with a spirit of excellence.

It didn't matter if they liked me. It only mattered that they could depend on me to do my job. I understood that early from my upbringing and my days in the Air Force. His comments, though eye-opening, were not going to dissuade me from my opportunity. With an unseen chuckle to myself, I thought, *They will work for me one day.*

My family and my life experiences had prepared me for what I experienced in Evansville. My parents and grandparents had taught me that life was not particularly kind to Black folks, and my family instilled in me a sense of strength and resiliency. My grandparents were not ones to dwell on the ills of the world, but they shared stories of the discriminatory practices they had to overcome. Yet they remained people of deep faith with humility and openness to all.

One story they told was of their desire to buy land in rural northern Michigan. At the time, no one was selling land to Black people. It wasn't illegal. It was only the racist practices of the time. They tried to purchase land on several occasions and were turned away. Never ones to quit, they had to develop another plan.

They had befriended a white man who agreed to represent them to complete the purchase. Finally, they were successful. The lesson I learned was that other people cannot determine your fate. With commitment, relentlessness, and a willingness to approach a challenge from different angles, you can accomplish what you want.

I learned the lesson and applied it. It helped me effectively handle that coworker and would become a cornerstone of how I approached my career and my life. That comment would be the only time I was directly told how unwelcome I was, but I would live through countless microaggressions from others simply because I was a woman of color (WOC).

Whether it was the comments about how different I was from other Black people, my aggressiveness, how well I spoke, or the fascination with my ever-changing hairstyles, there was always an undercurrent that somehow I had been let into a place that should have never opened the door for me or for those who look like me.

My thirty years as a public sector employee would be filled with many firsts. I was aware that I was shattering glass ceilings along the way. However, my ultimate focus remained on doing great work. In the process, I established a reputation for delivering, and I caught the attention of colleagues who would support, encourage, and invest in my career, much like my grandparents' friend, who opened the door for them to buy the land they wanted.

My network opened doors for me and positioned me to begin opening doors for other people. While my career skyrocketed, I was cognizant that very few women of color were having the same career success.

This lack of women of color would be undeniable on Tuesday, August 9, 2022, at 5:30 p.m. I sat in my home office in Washington, DC, catching up on emails after spending another exhausting day of back-to-back Zoom meetings. I know the exact time because it is captured in an email exchange.

During that time, I was the second in command, leading a geographically dispersed organization of over thirty-one thousand employees, and I had been invited to a speaking engagement. In preparation to represent the organization, I reviewed the current organization diversity statistics for the upcoming breakfast panel, where I would be addressing an internal organization of the National Black Employee Association.

Reviewing the data, I saw approximately thirty-one thousand employees, approximately fifty-nine hundred women, and—there it was in black and white—954 Black women. I couldn't help it. I performed a quick calculation in my head and realized that 954 represented less than *three percent* of the total population of employees in the organization. At that moment, my heart shattered, and I responded to that email, "Nine hundred and fifty-four Black women, it breaks my heart," to which the receiver, a strategic communications specialist, replied, "I'm sorry, Angela. It really is sad." She was correct.

No one celebrates these women or tells the stories of those who made it against the odds. Their careers could be defined as a nightmare filled with overt and covert racism, sexual harassment, and a prevailing sense of hopelessness. Yet there is beauty in their triumph over the challenges they faced. They have been the unheard and unseen among us. The time had come to write about the impact of these women of color in the public sector. I always knew I would write this book, and seeing the numbers on my computer screen became the proverbial camel's back. My silence was broken.

As a scholar and practitioner with a keen interest in public sector organizations and leadership for women of color, I recognized the current research and writing was focused on women of color in corporate and educational settings but was silent on the impact of women in broader public sector workspaces. How do these women move into the senior leadership positions? What can their success teach future generations? How can you apply these teachings to impact your career?

According to the Census of Governments, Survey of Public Employment & Payroll Summary Report: 2022 approximately 19.2 million persons are employed by state and local governments combined (Saxon et al. 2023). A report by the Equal Employment Opportunity Commission (EEOC) in 2021 stated there were 5,327,812 full-time women and minorities employed in local and state governments. Women of color that make it to the top positions of officials and administrators is 14.6 percent of that number (EEOC 2021). In 2020, 2.1 million persons worked for the federal government (EEOC 2020). Of those, women make up 44.44 percent of the workforce and hold 37.85 percent of the senior executive service (SES) positions, the highest federal rank. The ethnicity of women in the SES ranks is not broken out, but people of color account for 22.8 percent of SES members (Office of Personnel Management 2022).

The US is experiencing increased population growth, and it is expected that people of color will experience the greatest increases in the workforce through 2050. This change means the makeup of the public sector workforce is changing (Riccucci 2021, 3, 5). Of the approximately twenty-one million people employed by the government, only a small percentage of the executive and professional ranks are women of color.

On top of that, "Women continue to face a number of challenges in the workplace including, for example, sexism, gender stereotypes, microaggressions, unequal pay, family responsibilities discrimination (FRD) and race or color discrimination" (Riccucci 2021, 101). With the continued growth of WOC entering public sector positions, there is no reason to believe things will change. In fact, without change, the situation will get worse. We must intentionally work to eradicate the barriers that keep all women from entering public service and keep them trapped in specific career fields and lower-paying jobs.

After spending more than thirty years in the federal government and the military and rising to the senior executive service (SES), I look around and still see very few people who look like me. For women of color, the playing field is not level. However, it *is* possible for a woman of color to reach the senior executive service rank in the public sector, and the women featured in this book will show you how.

You'll learn about the first African American female Fire Chief of Prince George's County and the first Latina female assistant superintendent of a public school district in Harrisburg, Pennsylvania. You'll find a common thread in each of their stories. Even after they've invested in their education, completed certifications, and taken the jobs that others didn't want, without help, they would not have reached the executive ranks.

I, too, have been sponsored and have also mentored and networked with other women and helped them to reach senior positions. All our stories led me to this: The way to fast-track women's careers to senior positions in the public sector is through sponsorship, networks, and mentors.

Sponsors and mentors can lift you up or push you forward, but you must do the work.

This book is for:

- women of color who are starting their career and considering going into a leadership position
- women of color in middle management who want to seek a senior leadership position
- senior leaders who want to be a sponsor but don't know where to begin
- college women of color considering a career in public service
- anyone who wants to support women of color on their journey

- those who believe in the importance of women of color in key leadership positions to advance policies that create change and give voice to the marginalized
- women of color nearing retirement considering an encore career in public service

Join me on a transformative journey that will empower women of color to lead confidently in the public sector. Let's rewrite the narrative together. Keep reading and be part of the change.

# PART I

# HOW YOU SHOW UP

———

# CHAPTER 1

# FROM OUTSIDER TO TRAILBLAZER: EMBRACING AUTHENTIC LEADERSHIP

———

Strike one: You're an outsider. Strike two: You are not a controller. Strike three: We don't know you, and you just got here. Automatically, you should not be here. You are out, or that's what "they" thought.

Natasha Durkins or Tash's fifteen-year federal service journey began with the excitement of a new opportunity when she entered the agency from a contractor position. A year later, that excitement would turn to angst as she accepted her first promotion to a management position. Her new coworkers expressed surprise and disbelief at her selection. Those around her were adamant she was not qualified and that she must have known someone.

They did not know she had about ten years of management experience from the private sector, although it wouldn't have mattered to them because, as she says, in the "environment, not being a controller, you are immediately thought of as less than, particularly coming from outside of the agency. It was a bit of an uphill battle from the start."

To understand her leadership journey, we'll focus on her early experiences outside of the government, which framed her approach to life. "I worked at [the restaurant chain] Roy Rogers as a manager in Dupont Circle, which is a white-collar working area of DC, and people did not treat us well. I didn't like how people treated my team. I felt like they deserved a level of respect.

That's when I kind of started this crusade around valuing people who are in the service industry or whose job is primarily customer service or support. That has been a theme of my leadership ever since. It has also driven how I expect people to treat me." The treatment of people as human beings, just a basic level of respect based solely on the fact that we are human beings, would become one of Tash's values.

Her first promotion in the federal agency was not by chance. Her manager wanted someone who had not grown up in the culture. The team was responsible for implementing a new program, and things were not going well. Some broken relationships needed healing. Tash was the ideal candidate to lead the group through these complexities. She had some project management experience from the private sector, and most importantly, her manager "saw in me the ability to create those relationships."

The job was difficult. "It just felt like whatever direction I was going and the person I was talking to, I had to prove myself. All those different ways and it was exhausting. I also had basically argued why my perspective was valuable. It wasn't even just me just speaking up, but then once you spoke up, you had to convince everybody that your input was worth something. I remember wondering about a year into the management job if I was in the right place because I was just tired of going to meetings and having to just try to make my voice heard."

She didn't have a strong network yet, but one of the ways she survived this experience was with the help of a few colleagues. "I was fortunate in that a couple of Black men kind of wrapped their arms around me metaphorically and supported me because they knew more than I knew about how challenging it was going to be."

The constant fighting that Tash experienced caused her to shut down. She stopped voicing her opinion because she was anticipating the "argumentative approach to whatever I was saying that dismissiveness." She found herself sitting in meetings, "quietly having the same idea as others, but knowing that it wasn't gonna be received the same or well. So, I wouldn't necessarily say it." These struggles did not stop Tash. She led her team and accomplished the goals, which led to her next management position.

This may have been the most challenging experience yet. Tash found herself working for a Black woman who believed Tash was competition. The fact that the manager could only see the color of Tash's skin exacerbated the pain of this experience. She was experiencing colorism. Merriam-Webster.com defines colorism as "prejudice or discrimination especially within a racial or ethnic group favoring people with lighter skin over those with darker skin."

Tash recounted, "She believed everybody thought highly of me and liked me because I was a light-skinned woman." She made it clear that Tash brought no value to the position. This experience negatively impacted Tash's life. "I was high anxiety, some depression, I started feeling physically ill coming to work every Monday." It was such a toxic environment that Tash had to remove herself from it.

Though she described this situation as "devastating," she said, "I refused to let that impact my ability to have relationships with other Black women at the agency." Tash was raised in a predominately white environment, where she was too "white acting" for Black kids and too Black for the white cliques. She spent much of her childhood not fitting in, and because of this experience, she knew the importance of having relationships, especially with women who looked like her.

She applied for another position, and a guardian angel stepped in. "I ended up in a position where a man who's a controller... saw some value. I built up enough credibility that somebody recommended to him that he should hire me, and he did. He saw something in me, such that he would not allow me to continue sitting quietly. He helped me start finding my voice again. This new job gave me a new start."

She chuckled, and I could hear the joy in her voice. "I had found new life" working for this white man. "He pushed me and saw some value in my different perspective. He was finally someone I encountered who valued a diverse set of inputs from people. He did not just want to be sitting in a room with other controllers because he was a controller." His belief in her would reignite her passion for work. "He exposed me to new people and introduced me to people. He wanted to see my success. He became a strong advocate for me, which helped me then start reestablishing my own personal self-confidence and finding and using my voice again."

The power of someone seeing and believing in her gave her the courage to begin to show up. Tash wasn't expecting this level of support from him. He did not exhibit the pet-to-threat behaviors that are sometimes seen when a white man takes a Black woman under his wings, develops and exposes her, and then shuts her down if she is seen as too good. "The better I got, the more he supported and pushed me up and out. Then this started giving me another voice that I think is critically important to how I lead today."

As her confidence and relationship grew with her manager, they were able to discuss sensitive subjects and would have candid conversations, "including some of the microaggressions that we deal with today. Being able to talk with him candidly about it kind of gave me practice being able to speak with everybody about it now." These discussions prepared her to face racial and gender issues with grace and professionalism.

After a few years, that manager retired, and in came the new boss. Their relationship was a challenging one to build. Tash continued to excel in her position. However, things were not connecting for the two of them. She was doing all she could to support him to the point of exhaustion because she wanted his validation. "It literally took a good two years before he saw the value that I could offer him."

Tash had learned a valuable lesson. You cannot make people appreciate you and what you offer if they don't see it. No matter what she did, he couldn't see her. She stopped trying so hard, and what happened next was a surprise. "He was at my door asking for counsel and asking for input on things because I just stopped and let him do his thing. I stopped trying so hard to help him be successful. He felt it missing when I stopped, and that's when the value kicked in." This was the crossroads of the relationship, yet he had not developed a true belief in her.

She had an opportunity to temporarily run a large organization. Instead of his encouragement, he said, "I don't see you in that role." His lack of confidence showed Tash he didn't believe in her. She applied anyway and got the job. The position exposed her to new knowledge, opportunities, and networks. She enjoyed the experience so much that she applied for the same position in another state when it opened.

When she told her boss she was going to apply, he was still not a believer. He suggested who would get the role instead of her and further stated, "It's a slim chance you'll get it." Tash got the job, and once she did, he started to see her differently. Their relationship has a storied ending. He has since retired, but after she accepted an opportunity to lead an organization of approximately thirteen hundred people, he sent her a message. "He congratulated me and said, I remember the times when you were teaching me how to lead. If you just keep doing that, you'll be very successful."

As a woman of color, the challenges continue to show up. No matter how self-aware and confident you become, you must continue to do the work. Tash prepared to begin a meeting in a newly constructed conference room with beautiful white walls and a new gray rectangular conference table with new black mesh chairs around it. The meeting participants were a Black man and a white man from her agency as well as some older gentlemen from another agency.

As they entered the room, "they called out my colleague's name, said hello, shook his hand, looked at me, looked away, and just walked into the conference room. When I walked in, I introduced myself since they just walked away from me. I guess they thought I was his handler." The meeting began, and the guests were making eye contact and speaking directly to Tash's colleague while ignoring her.

After several minutes, "I stopped the meeting. I said, 'You know what, I'm sorry. Let's just pause the conversation for a moment. I would like to take a step back and provide some clarity. I don't think I explained our roles. Let me provide that clarity because that will help our conversation.' Then I explained what this colleague did and that I was going to approve this for the organization. They'd be reporting the status of this progress to me, and I would be responsible for the oversight so we could complete the mission for them. 'It's going to be important that you're engaging with them and me as we work through this process. Are there questions about that?' All of a sudden, I got eye contact from there on out. And when the thank-you note came after the meeting, it was addressed to me. I wouldn't have done that some years ago."

She attributed this experience to assumptions made by the gentlemen from the other agency. She was not sure if it was because she was a woman, a Black woman, or something else. Tash was not dressed in a typical dark business suit, as she was known for wearing bright, colorful clothing. She looked younger than she was, and she was a Black woman with naturally curly hair and a soft-spoken voice. "I couldn't possibly be the senior executive they had been waiting to meet."

She used this as a teachable moment. Tash was aware that this was likely to be the experience of the meeting. She told her colleague—Gary, a white man—ahead of time to watch what happened in the meeting. After the meeting, they discussed what transpired and Tash implored Gary to recognize when this behavior is happening and "be part of resolving the issue." It's important that others speak up, and changing this behavior is not solely the role of women of color. "I will no longer dismiss or overlook these things and just walk away angry and not address it. I'm going to address it."

Tash's communication style and ability to approach challenging conversations have become the hallmark of her leadership. It would be how she describes using her voice. It took her a while to find a comfortable style that was authentic to who she was as a person because she "was trying to figure out how to have good relationships with people that were actually built on something substantive." Each time she uses her voice, she becomes even clearer about who she is and what she values, crystallizing her authenticity.

## The Importance of Authenticity

A quick Amazon book search for the keyword "authenticity" returns over fifty thousand titles. It appears people are very interested in the topic of authenticity. What is it? In academia, several definitions of authenticity have been studied with no singular agreed-upon definition. I have chosen to define authenticity using the common components of each definition and summarized by Mengers: "An authentic person must have access to, accept, and act in accordance to their internal states, emotions, and thoughts, even if it goes against outside influences" (Mengers 2014, 20).

The study of authenticity began out of positive psychology. The previous president of the American Psychological Association, Martin Seligman, focused his work on how mindset impacted illness and disease, and here's how he defined positive psychology. "The field of positive psychology at the subjective level is about positive subjective experience: well-being and satisfaction (past); flow, joy, the sensual pleasures, and happiness (present); and constructive cognitions about the future—optimism, hope, and faith"

(Seligman 2002, 3). Martin's work wanted to move the field of psychology beyond illness and disease to include what makes people flourish (Seligman 2002; Mengers 2014). Much of the positive psychology research has focused on the well-being of individuals.

This research could be discussing me. My focus on my well-being never came into stronger focus than in 2005. In the summer of 2005, I had recently finished a year of chemotherapy and radiation treatment for my breast cancer diagnosis. I tried to make sense of my life but was struggling with mental, physical, and emotional exhaustion. My thoughts were unclear. My body wanted rest, and the unanswered questions lingered. What should have been an amazing time in my life was a time of despair.

Prior to my diagnosis in 2004, I had recently accepted an operations supervisor position in a twenty-four-hour air traffic facility and relocated my family from Detroit to northern Virginia. I was excited, hopeful, and ready to create a thriving work environment. I settled into my new position and began the work of learning about my team and the responsibilities of the new role.

Within the first six months of my position, I woke one morning to blood on my pillow. I checked my nose first, and there was no blood. I was shocked when I realized that a small scar left from a breast biopsy was bleeding. This moment changed everything about me and began a journey to eradicate the disease from my body. What I could not have known was the experience would cause me to reassess my values.

After treatment, a war raged in my head—a fight between the desire to stay in a position that I had worked to attain and the need to care for myself and reconnect to meaning in my life by stepping down and refocusing my energy. I also no longer had the passion and the energy to devote to my team. The work felt meaningless, and I knew that to stay in the role would be a disservice to my employees. After I made the difficult decision to step down, the challenge became how to tell the people who supported my career that I wanted out. How could I find a way home back to my roots in Detroit?

The decision represented a shift in my life from a career focus to an internal focus on self and an external focus on family. I believed going home would help me gain clarity and to help me process my experiences, but I was nervous. I contacted my previous sector manager in Detroit, and after small talk, I explained I could no longer serve the employees in my organization because I didn't have the energy.

"I need to come home," I said. "Do you have a position for me?"

He responded, "No, you should have contacted me sooner. I don't have any vacancies."

My heart sank into my stomach for a split second. Disappointment. Then I replied, "I couldn't have called you earlier because I didn't know I needed this. You do understand that if it's meant to be, I will return even if you don't have a position."

In that moment, I felt powerful and courageous. I was certain I would have the opportunity to return home, though I did not know how. I needed a plan, and after deliberation, I contacted my previous frontline manager in Detroit, who reported to the sector, and I discussed my desire to return home.

He and I shared a positive professional relationship that had been cultivated over a few years of working together. He was a compassionate leader who listened and connected to the experience I shared with him. He supported my desire, and with the support of the sector manager and working through the human resources staff, he created a position within the organization so I could return. Within a few months, I secured my old position and returned to Detroit.

The power of using my voice to advocate for myself and to openly express my thoughts without reservation is one of the ways I show up authentically. Speaking my truth in a way that others can receive it is a deeply held value. To do anything less would cause people to experience me as inauthentic and would impact how I lead my organization and form human connections. Much like Tash, the more I exercise my voice, my authenticity, the more confident I feel about who I am.

## Authentic Autonomy

I achieved my well-being by remaining true to who I am and sticking to my values of family, health, and self-care. While I didn't need the research to see it in action, studies have determined "how being oneself does relate positively to well-being" (Mengers 2014, 2). A structured literature review was conducted on published research on authenticity and uniqueness. "Preliminary evidence suggests that 'being yourself' does relate to well-being" (52). Authenticity shows a correlation with well-being (Mengers 2014). Its importance is that where there is well-being, there is less anxiety and depression. Individuals can exercise autonomy over their lives.

Martin Seligman, also known as the father of positive psychology, argues that psychology should build on humanistic concepts like authenticity to understand human flourishing scientifically. He contends psychological strategies amplifying strengths like authenticity could prove more beneficial to individuals than a solely correcting weakness (2002). Authenticity is relevant to positive psychology because research demonstrates its connection to well-being, and positive psychology seeks to scientifically understand and cultivate human strengths like authenticity to improve well-being. Mine and Tash's stories highlight the concept of authenticity and positive psychology.

Tash's next experience shows how being authentic helped her exercise autonomy over something most people don't want to talk about, much less address—menopause. She recounted an experience and giggled with childlike happiness about normalizing menopause in the workplace. After a particularly challenging night of sweats, Tash decided she was going to talk about it at work with her peer group.

With her color-coordinated fan waving back and forth in front of her face, she informed her colleagues—comprised of men and women—that she was hot. "I'm gonna be talking about this for a while. This is going to go on for a while, so just get used to it. If you see me fanning myself, I'm hot. You don't have to say, are you hot? We're going to start talking about this because a lot of us are going through it and feeling embarrassed because our face is suddenly sweating."

Using her voice to address a reality was a powerful act not only for women's feelings but also for the men who are not sure what to say or whether they should remain silent. It created space for conversation.

She has attributed her values in helping her find her voice and to "being in tune with myself because even when you're struggling to identify your top three to five values, you have to be willing to acknowledge when things don't feel right for you."

Like so many women, Tash would ignore her feelings. She would "dismiss it, push it down, kind of act like it wasn't there. Now, I let that thing rise on up and let it inform my steps, and sometimes those steps might need to find a better place or a different relationship. I would characterize a clear misalignment with my values." She had finally learned how to listen, accept, and follow her intuition.

CHAPTER 2

# BEYOND THE WALL: HARNESSING THE POWER OF VOICE

———

"It's been reported to me that I'm a ballbuster or that I can be a really strident bitch." Like the old Virginia Slims Menthol advertising slogan, she "had come a long way, baby."

Victoria Wei sat along the wall in a typical federal office building conference room where the drab cream walls hadn't seen a coat of paint in years. They'd excluded her from the conversation again. She sat quietly between coworkers, trying not to squirm in the old loud chairs for fear of drawing unwanted attention. As she looked around, she noticed a room full of "old white men" gathered around the long wooden conference table seated in black vinyl rolling chairs, speaking and "telling the younger people what to do. She was dismissed."

The weight of her anger grew heavier by the second. Victoria didn't know if they dismissed her because of her youth, because she was a woman, or for another reason.

Whatever the reason, she had grown tired of this scene playing out and took matters into her own hands.

She confidently sat at the conference table during the next meeting, perhaps unaware of traditional protocols and the "fearlessness of youth." The people in the room looked at her in disbelief with questioning eyes that asked, "Who is she?" Victoria had decided, "I would not be relegated to the wall or the window. I needed to be at the table." With a fire of determination in her belly, she dared anyone to tell her that she couldn't sit at the table. As agency counsel, she understood that her expertise was necessary.

This exclusion, the silencing of her voice, would play out throughout her twenty-year career, even as she had entered the executive service. At this point, she was at the table, but at times, others told her that she needed to get out of "their" seat and would stand over as they tried to intimidate her to move. She refused to get up because what could they do to her? She found the lack of repercussions for failing to move freeing. Finally, comfortable with herself and less concerned about what others thought of her, she had the confidence to think, "I am not moving, so get over it."

Victoria grew up in a predominately white neighborhood in a family that valued status and finances. She was Harvard-educated and earned her juris doctorate from Northwestern University. Her schooling was in white male communities and institutions. After graduating from law school, she practiced in the public sector for several years until she decided to detour. The pressure from her family—external expectations of others—to live a life aligned with their values caused her to go into private practice, believing it would satisfy their desires. She found that the work in those firms "did not speak to her soul." She burned out and left private practice.

She did not immediately return to the government. She wanted to do work she believed would "feed her soul." She performed as a voiceover artist for several years, recording commercials and audiobooks. She tried to remain hidden behind the camera because few roles were available in front of it for Asian Americans. At the time, she had a Western last name that opened doors for those jobs. Unfortunately, the work was unstable, so she returned to the government as an attorney.

After practicing law for five years, Victoria took a position that would change her career trajectory. She was fortunate to work for a woman who saw and encouraged her talent. Her initial role was that of a special assistant, a singular contributor role in an organization that could not have been more different from her role in the general counsel's office.

After successfully executing her duties, her manager told her "She needed a staff if she was going to move up in the world." Victoria enjoyed what she was doing, and though she was not a manager, she appreciated using the leadership skills of empowering others, using influence, and removing obstacles to complete the work. However, she didn't have plans to move up.

Her boss would evolve Victoria's special assistant position into that of a chief of staff with managerial responsibility. She encouraged Victoria to apply for the job, telling her, "She was meant to do it." Victoria did not believe it was meant to be. However, she states, "I was so loyal to her that I thought, okay, I'll try it. If this woman I admire tremendously tells me this is going to be good for me, I trust her, and I will try it." She applied and became a manager. Victoria found that she enjoyed managing people. "She had a knack for it." She served in this role for three years after her boss retired until a new manager took over.

During those three years, Victoria's confidence grew as she overcame obstacles and stereotypes. The microaggressions and offhanded comments like "Wow, your English is so good" happened often enough to become almost imperceptible white noise. She found that if she defied Asian stereotypes of being passive, soft-spoken, and not speaking her mind, she would "receive pushback and backlash." Because of her upbringing, community, and education, Victoria had an excellent command of English. That would be a determining skill that has led to her effectiveness as a leader.

Even so, Victoria often chose her words carefully to achieve precision while aiming for maximum impact. She recalls one time she had to collaborate with another organization to produce a response to Congressional inquiries. The other organization's employees provided information that was unresponsive and borderline misleading. After much deliberation, she responded as thoughtfully as possible, outlining the requirements of an effective response and encouraging the other employee to revise his response to be more informative.

The other employee's manager exploded at her, calling her condescending and accusing her of using her education and background to act superior to him and his employee. After that experience, Victoria realized that no matter how carefully she treaded, people would bring their baggage into her interactions. As a result, "I think over time, I become less concerned with how I am personally perceived and more concerned about how I stick up for what I think is right to do for the population I serve."

She learned to represent herself and those she led through her communication skills. Keenly aware that she was different, she communicated in a style that minimized those differences. She could mimic the cadence of people that she was talking to. "It's a socio-linguistic phenomenon that when you want to demonstrate an affinity with another person, you begin to adopt their mannerisms and their linguistic style unconsciously. What I have discovered is that if I do certain things, like punctuate my sentences the way they punctuate their sentences, it makes them feel more at ease." She described this phenomenon as "authentic code-switching."

Authentic to her because she found it was easy. For much of her life, Victoria found herself in environments where she was the only woman and the only Asian American. Growing up, few other Asian Americans lived near her, and she attended a predominantly white male Ivy League university. She developed a mechanism to help her survive and thrive. She applied this technique to "fit" in without losing herself.

The incoming manager, an African American man, pushed her out of her place of comfort. Having come from a background of overcoming obstacles, he quickly recognized her potential.

"What are you doing?" he asked. His question was more profound than its simplicity.

In Victoria's role, she orchestrated the running of his office. Her new manager immediately saw that her position "was not maximizing" her talents. Victoria didn't know what he was talking about.

She laughed in nervous disbelief. "No, no, I love doing this. I love solving problems. I love the tactical work. I love the day-to-day challenge and excitement of being a chief of staff. I love it. Please don't make me do anything else."

He was not the type of person you could tell no. A successful individual in his own right, he had been an enlisted member of the Air Force, who went on to receive his commission and ultimately retired as a two-star general. She thought he was amazing. He had paved his way despite adversity. He provided more than just offering a professional challenge—an invitation to amplify her voice.

Victoria accepted the new challenge, where she was no longer merely solving day-to-day tactical issues. She used her voice to shape the organization's future, mentor the next generation, and challenge systemic bias. Her story reminds us that regardless of our challenges, our voices can change, influence others, and ultimately shape our destinies. Like Victoria, using my voice would shape my career path and positively impact the lives of people around me.

"I was surprised when he asked me to be his mistress of ceremonies."

I received a hearty laugh from the attendees as I spoke those words as the MC at a luncheon for a retiring manager.

I had spent the early years of my career as an electronic technician working for a federal agency. My entry into this industry began when I served my country in the United States Air Force as an electronics technician, and now I was ready to advance my career.

In 2000, a vacancy for a frontline manager in my local area opened, and I applied for the position. It was a promotion, the first rung on my leadership journey, and the possibility and trepidation of the unknown excited me.

I worked in Michigan in a suburb of Detroit where only a few women and fewer women of color were employed. When I applied for the job, no other Black woman was in a leadership role in an organization geographically dispersed throughout Michigan. I was skeptical about my selection chances, yet I applied anyway.

I had no illusions that the job would be easy, nor did I believe that employees would readily accept me, but I knew I had to try. Employees in the organization were all men, and if that was not challenging enough, several of them were old enough to be my father or grandfather. Now the question became: How would I win them over?

The sector manager selected me for the position and another Black woman as a second-level manager. They were the final selections he made before his retirement and were significant. To my knowledge, no other Black women or women of color held those roles in Michigan. I was excited to become a manager, but healthy nervousness tempered that excitement.

Before his departure, I had a chance to chat with the outgoing manager. He expressed his belief in my ability to be successful and commented that he wished he would be around to support me. I would come to wish that, too.

In my first year as a manager, I experienced a full range of emotions as I worked to create a team environment. As I reflect, at times inside I was experiencing a drive down Lombard Street in San Francisco, often thought of as the most crooked street, but on the outside, I was calm in the storm. I felt the pride of team accomplishment and the disappointment of failure. Overall, I was pleased with what I had accomplished.

My end-of-year performance discussion with my boss was meaningless and colored with the tropes often leveled at Black women. There I was—a first-year manager expecting meaningful feedback to help me improve and grow—and I received generic commentary lacking any substance.

Roger said I was doing well and identified one area for improvement. He said that, at times, "I was too aggressive." I was surprised because I hadn't been made aware of any instances of that behavior during the year, nor could I recall an event where I believed I had displayed that type of behavior. I asked him if he could provide specific instances of my aggressive behavior. I was seething inside. However, I sat there looking directly at him.

Roger sat quietly for a moment from behind his desk, his eyes darting around the room with an occasional look at me. I imagine he was thinking about how to respond or was shocked that I had asked the question. Either way, he said, "No, I can't think of a specific example."

I sat silently, thinking, *I know you can't because that is not how I have shown up.* The room was thick with tension, and my temperature continued to rise. I was angered that my manager would easily categorize me as an "aggressive Black woman," a stereotype that rolled off his tongue like an indisputable law of nature. How should I respond?

I calmly replied, "In the future, when providing me feedback, please provide specific examples. I like to reflect on my feedback, and with examples, I can analyze what I was thinking or doing at the time and then determine if I need to change or if my behavior was appropriate." Roger sat there a bit stunned and said, "Okay."

Maintaining my composure, I added, "Also, it would help if you would not ignore me when you pass me in the hall in the morning." I recounted instances where I had walked past him and spoken, and he didn't bother to look my way or to respond.

Roger gave me what I believed to be a flimsy excuse that he was distracted and didn't hear me. Women of color and Black women are often overlooked and unseen in the workplace, which are forms of marginalization. Too often, these women are afraid to address these issues for fear of repercussions (Thomas et al. 2021). I would not allow him to devalue me as a human or minimize my impact on accomplishing organizational goals. Nor was I going to allow him to excuse his behavior.

I didn't care about his response, and his opinion was inconsequential. What mattered to me was that I had notified him of the treatment I expected, and I was not allowing him to label me. I was taking a stand. This was my first year as a manager and became the foundation of how I would show up authentically as a leader. Voicing the truth served me continuously throughout my career as I accepted progressively senior leadership positions.

## Why Your Voice Matters

It's no secret that women are interrupted, ignored, and over-talked in meetings. Their ideas are stolen or, worse yet, told that the idea makes no sense. This consistent level of engagement for women in the workplace is causing women to shut down. When the few women are not speaking up and engaging, we're missing meaningful perspectives and  viewpoints.

For women, a critical part of advancing in your career is learning how to use your voice to speak up, engage, and be heard in conversations. Historically, women are often overlooked because they are the only ones at tables full of men.

Recent research suggests that men dismiss women's viewpoints as irrelevant or emotional when engaging in discussions. Men claim women don't have facts, data, or analytics to support their decisions. These common thoughts make it easy for men to sit in meetings and discount women, just like they did to Victoria.

But we must consider something beyond that. In Deborah Tannen's article, "The Power of Talk: Who Gets Heard and Why," she states, "How we talk and listen are deeply influenced by cultural experience. Although we might think that our ways of saying what we mean are natural, we can run into trouble if we interpret and evaluate others as if they necessarily felt the same way we'd feel if we spoke the way they did" (1995).

One of those things is that men and women communicate very differently, and how we communicate begins in childhood. Girls generally are in environments where they're taught to be more congenial and get along. Boys often play sports where they compete with one another very early on, asserting their dominance. So, as the two genders grow up, they grow up very differently in some aspects that play out in the workplace.

In other words, different cultures, experiences, and backgrounds will understand terms differently. Words have meaning informed by your lived experience. The article further goes on to state that linguistic style often impacts how people communicate and understand each other. Tannen states that "linguistic style is a set of culturally learned signals by which we not only communicate what we mean but also interpret others' meanings and evaluate one another as people" (1995).

This also poses a problem for women of color. Whether you're an African American, Latina, Asian American, or Pacific Islander, cultural norms of your environment, ethnicity, or religion come into play. Learned communication skills impact the work environment. If women have grown up in these norms, it certainly makes it challenging to operate outside of their standards in a work environment. Also, one set of stereotypes is so prevalent that people generally assume the stereotype is accurate. For example, as a Black woman, I am assertive. However, I am labeled angry and aggressive, which comes from stereotyping. For more information on stereotypes, see Chapter 6.

The other issue is that women's personal communication norms don't align with the accepted leadership practices. The way we view effective communication is based on the traditional communication style of men. Generally, men can engage in spirited and robust dialogue, often disagreeing with each other with vigor. If you've ever been in an environment where many men are involved in a discussion, you know it can be lively with a lot of energy.

The conversation can be loud and filled with testosterone as they banter back and forth. They can have a spirited debate and then go out for a dry gin martini. However, it can be challenging for women to join in those conversations and provide feedback. Their voices are easily drowned out, making it difficult for them to engage in meaningful discourse.

We understand those cultural norms at play are critical for women. As you progress in your career, it's crucial to understand your communication style. Effective communication involves the words you choose, your mindset, and the teachings you have received on the subject. You should question whether your communication style is suitable for the environment you're in. Furthermore, if you have learned to stay quiet or believe it's wrong for women to voice their opinions, participating in essential leadership conversations will prove difficult.

Tannen highlights two critical elements we know about communication. One is that the words that we use have familiar meanings, but what is less visible to us is that "language also negotiates relationships" (1995). Through ways of speaking, we signal and create the relative status of speakers and their level of rapport. How we speak again suggests the level of authority we have. It also suggests how we see ourselves. Others can pick up on those created signals. They will tell people whether or not you're comfortable and whether you are coming across as competent.

In the article "Women, Find Your Voice," Heath, Flynn, and Holt offer some key things women can do to help with the phenomenon of being overlooked and underheard. One key takeaway is that women must get comfortable with conflict (2014). In many of these senior-level meetings, they debate ideas because of different opinions. When they feel strongly, they have a lot of energy expressing it, creating a lot of energy in the room and creating conflict.

To the extent that you can feel comfortable in that environment, your voice can be heard. I always say that professionals debate ideas. If the conflict concerns the concept, it should be a comfortable space. I think conflict or discomfort should only come up if someone is attacking you. If the discussion turns personal, that becomes a problem. Get comfortable with conflict.

Another critical thing women can do to increase being heard and seen is to get comfortable discussing before the meeting (Heath, Flynn, and Holt 2014). Take a look at your schedule. What is the upcoming agenda? What is the topic of the meeting? Is it a meeting for decision-making? Is it to come up with a new strategy? Is it just for discussion and sharing of new ideas? You have to figure out the intent of the meeting. Then, think about your position on the topic. Consider the positions of those members who will be at that meeting. Who is most likely to have a similar position to yours?

I recommend that you meet with them to determine where you have areas of agreement, and then, based on that agreement, you may develop a strategy so that when you walk into the room, both of you agree to support one another. You can amplify that person's idea, or they can amplify yours. You must seek an ally to help you make your voice and opinions heard. Tannen highlights another way to be heard in "Women, Find Your Voice." Preparation is the key (1995). Before meeting, write down key ideas to stay focused on the positions you plan to present.

The women highlighted in this chapter refused to be silenced. Instead, they have chosen to use their voices to share their expertise and speak their truth. It's your turn. Use your voice not just as a tool but also as a weapon, guiding light, and a bridge to challenge stereotypes and reshape the narrative.

## CHAPTER 3

# HAIR, IDENTITY, AND POWER: OWNING YOUR TRUE SELF AT WORK

---

"'Tone it down, Katrina.' I heard that a lot. 'You're too outspoken. Your appearance is too much with the hair. You know, you're bossy. You're argumentative, an angry Black woman.' I said, oh, so when my passion comes through, I'm angry. The 'tone it down' told me to just turn down my personality, and I have a big personality anyway."

They wanted her to conform to how society says you should look and speak. She would not contort herself to fit their mold or show up as anything less than who she was. This desire to be her true self was a nonnegotiable value underpinning her life.

Katrina, an industrial engineer by education, had spent her thirty-one-year career serving the American public. She was an outspoken, introverted Black woman known for her ever-changing hairstyles. One day, she had an afro; the next, braids or dreadlocks. Raised by a parent who was a long-time government employee, Katrina thought that since the military was not for her, she could serve in another way.

Her career began as a civilian working for the Department of the Navy. After ten years of working for the Navy, she accepted her first leadership role. It was not a managerial role but a team lead position. They asked her to take the job because she worked with people and had developed the expertise needed for the role. The position did not include any additional pay. "I just became the go-to girl for just getting things done. It made me feel good to bring people together."

Katrina eventually left the Navy position because it was apparent she would not advance. She was an "outsider," and this was the "good-old-boy club." The quality of her work didn't matter. They refused to promote her.

She didn't deal with "overt" discrimination, but it was clear: "My cousin's friend's brother's gonna get this job. And it doesn't matter if you're better at the job. As a matter of fact, we'd like you to stay so you can do all the work. But we're not going to promote you even though you are doing a great job."

After leaving the Department of the Navy, Katrina began working for the Federal Aviation Administration (FAA). Again, she would distinguish herself as a subject matter expert. "I love being the person people come to for these answers. I didn't want to get into management because, to me, that meant conforming."

She continued developing her leadership skills. "I had been doing a lot of building my leadership style, who I wanted to be, how I wanted to lead." She knew she liked leading, but "I stayed in my little niche and made it work" because she thought she would have to become someone else to be accepted. After approximately seven years, she received a management position.

The promotion was the path laid out in her career field. She enjoyed the work. However, she was often the only woman and the only African American woman. She found that while she didn't experience overt racism, she did experience racial microaggressions. For example, during an office potluck lunch, a coworker asked Katrina if she could make fried chicken. Another example occurred while sitting at the leadership table when asked by one of her peers to take the minutes. Katrina replied, "I took them last time. Somebody else can take them." Her colleague replied, "You don't have to be like that about it. I was just asking." Her colleague's response suggested she had no right to push back.

Aware that people thought she was "too outspoken," she thoughtfully crafted her responses and engagement. She realized every comment didn't require a response. "You could call it going along to get along. You could call it selling out. I couldn't go in with everything being a fight. I would pick my battles to what I think would be the most impactful. It's always that balancing act, and you're always on a tightrope trying to balance. Am I gonna say something this time, or am I gonna hold my tongue?"

When an executive position opened, she was not planning to apply until a colleague told her they would put someone over her to tell her what to do if she didn't take the job. Katrina decided to "take the plunge" and apply because it was important "how I wanted to be thought of and who my boss was going to be." She has found joy in her executive journey. "I love that I could see gaps somewhere and just say I want to go and fill that gap and lead."

In her executive positions, the microaggressions have lessened, but they still exist. "I felt like I had to be 110 percent just to be seen as a B plus." She handled the comments that she attributed to being a woman. "Can you be the one to organize the Christmas party?" She responded, "No, I am not that great at organizing. So no, get somebody else to do it." She had found "her voice."

Along with her voice, she learned the importance of having a support network. "Coming up in the ranks, I had nobody. I was trying to navigate and figure it out all by myself." She did not have that type of support throughout her career at the FAA. She had family, church, and community, but they didn't always understand what was important to her, and they didn't understand her work environment. Building a network took a long time because few other people looked like her, and she was naturally insular.

She has that network now, and it has created a safe space. "I am in a sorority, but it's nothing like having somebody in the moment when these things are happening. That's why I think it's important that people see women and women of color in these leadership positions. Building a network of colleagues is different than just women or any other kind of network. To me, it's just so powerful to call my sister down to my office and unload. Find your network of a few trusted agents and learn from their experiences."

The last twenty-five years of her life have changed her and helped her develop a strong sense of self. When she was younger, she wanted "people to think she was smart and to like her." Now, she has matured into a woman who knows she's smart and is no longer seeking external validation. "I carry myself and expect you to treat me a certain way. Act the way you want to be treated. I really believe that's true."

## Strong Sense of Self Defined

A strong sense of self refers to an individual's self-awareness, self-confidence, and self-esteem. It involves having a clear and accurate understanding of one's own beliefs, values, strengths, weaknesses, and personality traits. People with a strong sense of self are generally secure in their identity and are less likely to be influenced by other's opinions or expectations.

Having a strong sense of self allows individuals to make decisions that align with their values and goals so they can take responsibility for their actions. It also enables them to cope better with challenges and setbacks as they have a solid foundation of self-awareness and self-confidence to draw upon. Developing a strong sense of self is an ongoing process that involves self-reflection, self-discovery, and personal growth. It requires a willingness to confront one's fears, vulnerabilities, and limitations and an openness to learning and change.

Micha Goebig writes, "Close to 80 percent of women struggle with low self-esteem and shy away from self-advocacy at work," according to a study conducted by the National Bureau of Economic Research (2022). While low self-esteem is not necessarily the opposite of a strong sense of self, it can be a barrier to developing one. Low self-esteem is a negative perception of oneself and one's abilities, while a strong sense of self is a positive and confident understanding of oneself.

Someone with low self-esteem may struggle to feel confident in their skills or worthy of respect, making it more challenging to develop a strong sense of self. Imagine attending a meeting with colleagues, and you are the only woman of color in attendance. You have ideas that would benefit the project.

Instead, you remain silent, overwhelmed with the story playing in your head. "I'm not good enough. They might judge my comments." You leave the meeting plagued with what-ifs. This is an example of low self-esteem.

Now, picture yourself in the same session, engaged and fully expressing your ideas without regard to what people think. You understand that you bring value to the discussion, and "their" stereotyping does not stop you, much like Katrina when she refused to take the meeting minutes.

Developing a strong sense of self is a process that can involve overcoming obstacles like low self-esteem. You can build a stronger sense of self by working to improve self-esteem through self-care, therapy, and self-reflection. I should know. I thought I had to be someone else to be accepted.

Two moments stand out for me in my career when I allowed other people's perspectives and other people's isms to impact how I showed up at work. I was an electronics technician in my early twenties at the beginning of my career. There was no denying I was female, no matter how hard I tried to hide it. Yes, I was smaller, but I always had hips. I was a curvy girl, uncomfortable in my skin and afraid to stand out because of my shape.

One important thing for me was that I didn't want co-workers to see me as other. I was in an environment working with predominantly male technicians, and I wanted to be seen as one of the guys or maybe just not different, so I downplayed what would be considered "female" traits.

Even if I had wanted to wear pumps and a business suit, I would've been out of place, and it was in an environment where you wore jeans, sweatshirts, and sneakers to work anyway. I went out of my way to ensure I wore oversized hoodies, jeans, and combat boots, and I did not wear makeup. I remember wearing small earrings that you could barely see.

I thought I wanted to be successful in what I was doing, and I bought into this idea that to be successful, I had to fit in like the men I worked with. It wasn't who I was because I was a vibrant individual outside of work. Even in my discomfort with my physical body, I embraced my femininity with my colorful clothing, open-toed shoes, fitted jeans, and the occasional mini skirt. The only role models around me were men at work, so I fell in line.

I knew I needed to learn more and would have to learn from my colleagues. They may have been less willing to help train me if they saw me as a female. Worse yet, they may not have trusted my skills when working with me to resolve problems in the systems we maintained. This discourse happened in my head.

When I reflect, that was the environment. I made an intentional decision to try and separate my career from my true self. There's power in owning the decision to fit in with colleagues. The problem is that I thought I had to make that decision to be a valued team member. I showed up that way for a few years. I accomplished fitting in and learning from my colleagues, but those few years of hiding my body made me dislike my physical body even more.

The second instance came about eight years later in my career. I was still an electronics technician promoted to the Technical Support Unit. I had decided to embrace more of my femininity now. In the Technical Support Unit, you didn't have to always have on jeans and sneakers. I could be more feminine by wearing the occasional skirt, suit, and pumps, but I was usually dressed like my peers.

At this point, I was feeling more like myself, and I decided I was going to embrace my natural hair fully. I stopped chemically straightening my hair and began growing locs, or dreadlocks. Now, I was feeling bold and powerful and embracing this decision, and at the same time, suddenly, that fear came back about being accepted. What was I doing?

I was already "other" now. I was really going to be "other" with my hair in an environment with all men. When you start growing locs from short hair, they're tiny coils, and as they begin to lengthen, they take on a life of their own. Growing locs is akin to raising your children. They start as small twists. The coils then reach a point where they're like teenagers and become unruly. They're hard to control, and they stand on your head and wave in the wind.

"I have gone too far. I can't wear my hair like this in the environment. It is not acceptable. I'm going to stand out." Again, it did not fit into the traditional norms of what I believed it meant to be professional in the work environment. How did I handle it? I consciously chose to wear my hair covered with a scarf for several months. Now, that was outside of what we believe is traditional professional hairstyling.

I covered my hair so no one would see it standing up, and I wouldn't have to stand out. Nor would I have to feel embarrassed when people asked me about my hair. That also was a decision that was not owning who I was. I decided to deny my true self because of what people would think. It's another instance where those are not the decisions I should have had to make.

When you're a woman of color in these predominantly white male environments, you deal with stereotyping. How will people see and experience you? Are they willing to connect with you and help you as solid colleagues? You want to avoid alienating yourself from the team, but hiding your true self to fit in becomes exhausting.

There came a turning point. I can't tell you that there was a specific moment. I had an epiphany, a time when I could not continue hiding who I was. There are not enough baggy clothes to hide my female shape. I'd decided to wear my hair in a certain way. I owned that decision. It was a shift from lower self-esteem.

That was the true opportunity to own my sense of self. I was about nine or ten years into my career, and I had already established myself as a professional. People knew what to expect of me. I had already built a brand of getting in early, working hard, delivering, and being a team player.

I believed my career brand of how I worked would outshine what I looked like. I owned all of me. My work attire was colorful and professional. I let my locs loose, and some days, they stood on my head and flopped in the wind. I just laughed and went with the flow. It was what it was.

I would no longer try to fit into stereotypical molds of who people thought I should be and how I should look. I chose to show up as the professional I knew I was and do the best job possible. That's what I did. I focused on the work and no longer what people thought about me. That's what it means to have a strong sense of self. I was exercising agency over my being. I had comfort in knowing what I brought to the table. I let that speak for itself.

## Importance of a Strong Sense of Self

A strong sense of self can be vital for women of color in the workplace, where they may face unique challenges such as discrimination, microaggressions, and stereotypes. Here are a few ways a strong sense of self can help women of color at work:

1. Increase resilience: Women of color may face more obstacles and challenges in the workplace than their white counterparts. A strong sense of self can help you cope with these challenges more effectively and bounce back from setbacks.

2. Improve decision-making: Women of color with a strong sense of self are likelier to make decisions aligned with their values and interests rather than feeling pressure to conform to societal or workplace norms.

3. Greater self-advocacy: A strong sense of self can help women of color feel more confident in speaking up for themselves and asserting their needs and boundaries in the workplace.

4. Increase sense of belonging: Women of color may feel isolated or excluded in predominantly white workplaces. A strong sense of self can help them feel more grounded and secure in their identity while feeling less affected by feelings of imposter syndrome or other insecurities.

5. Improve mental health: Experiencing discrimination and microaggressions at work affects mental health. Developing a solid sense of self can help women of color maintain a positive self-image and resist internalizing negative messages.

6. Navigating microaggressions: A strong sense of self can shield against the daily microaggressions women of color often face in the workplace. For example, an Asian American woman told she's "good at math" as if it's a trait inherent to her ethnicity. A strong sense of self allows her to navigate such comments without internalizing stereotypes.

7. Career advancement: Women of color often face a "double glass ceiling" due to gender and racial biases. Advocating for your worth, as Katrina did, can help advance your career despite systemic barriers.

Building a strong sense of self is a lifelong journey that requires effort and commitment. However, it is a powerful tool for women of color when navigating workplace challenges and working toward achieving their goals. Here are some steps you can take to build a stronger sense of self:

1. Engage in self-reflection: Take time to reflect on your thoughts, feelings, and behaviors. Adapted from Powell (2009). Ask yourself questions like:
   "What are my values?"
   "What motivates me?"
   "What are my strengths and weaknesses?"

This can help you gain a deeper understanding of yourself. For example, if you are a Native American woman, understanding the values of community and tradition in your culture can help you leverage these in a corporate setting.

2. Practice self-acceptance: Accept yourself for who you are, including your flaws and imperfections. Treat yourself with compassion, kindness, and respect.
3. Set goals: Identify goals aligned with your values and interests. Having clear goals can give you a sense of direction and purpose.
4. Develop your skills and talents: Explore your interests and develop your skills and talents. Following this approach

can aid you in building confidence and achieving your goals.

5. Surround yourself with encouraging and supportive people: Practicing this can boost your confidence and make you feel more validated.

6. Take care of your physical and mental health: Taking care of your physical and mental health can help you feel more confident and resilient. This involves prioritizing sleep, nutrition, and exercise while possibly seeking help.

7. Set boundaries: Learn to say no to tasks that are not your responsibility, especially those stereotypically "feminine" or "ethnic," like organizing office parties or serving as the unofficial translator for other employees.

Remember, this process takes time and effort. "Becoming an individual with a strong sense of self and confidence is important for success. Understanding the value of one's personal choices, surroundings, and people that influence career success is essential" (Powell 2009).

Both Katrina's and my strong sense of self became our brand. People knew what to expect when they engaged with us. Katrina was unwavering in living in any way that did not honor her entire self, yet she acknowledges that even in her nonconformity, she wanted respect. I always knew who I was and chose to mask my true self for fear that others wouldn't accept me and because my authentic self did not fit the mold of the predominately white space. It became exhausting to keep hiding, but finally, I knew there was no other option than to be me and to be comfortable in my MEness!

# Final Thoughts on Natural Hair

The struggle to embrace our natural hair is a shared experience. For generations, we were told that our hair, in its natural state, was ugly, nappy, and unprofessional. I used to have relaxed hair, and I loved it when it was wrapped, flat ironed, and bumped. It made me feel good about myself. Unfortunately, society has placed systems that tell us our natural hair is unattractive and make it unwelcome in some spaces. Written policies disallow braids, locs, and twists. Sometimes, even afros are unwelcome. This politicization of hair has affected Black women, and it is disheartening to see that we have to have legislation such as the Crown Act to ensure that we can wear our hair the way it grows out of our scalp without fear of discrimination.

## CHAPTER 4

# FROM VISION TO REALITY: CRAFTING YOUR CAREER ROADMAP

---

Putting food on the table for her husband and children was at the forefront of her mind.

When Toni Washington graduated from Savannah State University, a Historically Black College and University in Georgia, she began a temporary position that eventually became permanent at the State Fire Marshal's office. In that role, she met many fire chiefs and learned about the different fire departments around the state.

She served in an administrative role and was often approached about working for the fire department because they had a focus on hiring more women and women of color. However, she was initially uninterested. "I was recruited by an African American male fire chief, who was the fire chief in the city of East Point. There were many times he and I had one-on-one conversations. He would always say you should come be a firefighter. No, not me. Of course, when I found myself without a job, with a husband and a child, I had to find out how I was gonna put food in their mouths. I had to do something."

When she began in the fire service, there were initially no women. Toni said, "There are over four hundred thousand paid career firefighters in the US, and women only make up 11 percent of that number. Black women make up 3 percent of the 11 percent of women." The fire chief "was working hard to try and get women, so I was one of the first seven women hired in the city of East Point here in Georgia."

According to the African American Firefighter Museum (2023), "Women have played a major role in the fire service ever since the 1800s when a slave named Molly Williams served as a volunteer firefighter in New York City."

Toni did not know what to expect in her new role. "I did really go into it blindly, not understanding the whole magnitude or the responsibility of the job. I thought I would go in there and get an office job and just cruise right along. I was naive." She quickly learned she was a minority and in the minority.

"I joke often, but there is some truth to it. As a Black woman on the back of a fire truck, and my hair doesn't work like that." Toni meant by that statement that most Black women's hair would go from straight to a coily afro with water and humidity, or the wind would destroy her hairstyle while she was riding on the back of a fire truck. She knew she wasn't long for that type of firefighting. If you know Black women, you don't mess with their hair, period.

"I decided my goal was to get to the top and to get to the top quickly. I created a roadmap, which I would not cruise down the road but accelerate down the road very quickly to ensure I reached the right level to be in charge." Once in charge, she wouldn't have to ride on the back of the fire truck.

Toni credits her career planning and thinking to what she learned at her alma mater, Savannah State. The schooling prepared her for what she faced. She learned about the high expectations and standards that come with the job. She knew it would not be easy from day one, so she prepared herself accordingly. She went back to school and earned her master's degree while continuing to work in the fire service.

Her guide for professional development was the handbook, which helped her climb the ranks. She quickly applied for any available opportunities, even if she didn't meet all the prerequisites. She also joined firefighting organizations such as the International Association of Black Professional Firefighters and Women in Fire, which provided her with support and training opportunities. All these efforts helped her exceed expectations and succeed in her career.

The intentional focus on getting ahead would only come with personal sacrifice. Her "daughter suffered" because Toni was studying and preparing and, at times, couldn't be involved in some of her activities. Her marriages suffered, and she endured two divorces. "I knew I had to be better than every male firefighter. If I weren't better than them, I would not have that opportunity."

As Toni reflected, she realized that "probably a lot of what I was putting on myself was self-inflicted as I look back today, but it had to be done for me to get where I am today." It was, as they say, the price of admission because "it's hard being in a male-dominated field to move forward."

Maneuvering (or promotion) in the fire service was not easy, mainly because there is a deep organizational history, "culture and traditions that you don't understand when you come in blindly." Toni entered the fire service with a few mentors. Because she worked at the state marshal's office, she qualified for and joined the International Association of Black Professional Firefighters. As a member of the organization, she heard about the obstacles that Black firefighters faced and how they overcame them.

Several of the Black male firefighters who were members of the Association guided her through her early career, which helped her succeed. One of those men was A. D. Bell, "the first and only African American state fire marshal in Georgia." Without mentors, many of the women who enter the fire service quit. They don't understand the culture, and they aren't welcome. There have been and continue to be "challenges with racism and sexism."

At times, Toni wanted to quit. The first time she considered leaving happened "one morning, and I was still working on the truck, not in a leadership position yet, and finding a noose hanging in the locker room, the bunker room right near my locker. I thought, I don't need this." She questioned why she was dealing with this.

As an educated woman, she knew her skills were portable, and she could find work elsewhere. She knew, "God put me on this earth for a reason, and I have to make sure I am fulfilling that obligation because he has created a lot of opportunities for me." She would not give up.

Toni eventually found an official mentor. She met Rosemary Cloud, the first African American woman fire chief in the United States. Rosemary served in the city of East Point and became Toni's mentor and eventually her boss. Rosemary continued Toni's development in preparation for her to become a fire chief one day. That day came.

"Chief Washington joined the City of Decatur in January 2009 as the first African American and first female to serve as the Fire Chief/Emergency Manager" (Women in Fire 2023).

"There have only been fourteen of us in the history of the fire service. I think right now it's about maybe six of us active." Some still don't see and respect you even when you get to the top. The challenges and the barriers are real from employees to vendors. "When I first became fire chief, vendors would come in, wanting to give sales presentations, and just refuse to recognize me as the fire chief." Toni described one instance when a vendor ignored her and spoke directly to her male subordinate employee. She was sure that the vendor knew that she was the fire chief. Instead of fighting every battle, she decided to listen to her mentor, A. D. Bell, and walk off when that happened.

"I keep going because the legacy I want to leave behind is to make sure I have created opportunities for people of color and women that weren't there before."

Toni has reached the pinnacle of her career, but she is community-minded and gives back through her work with her sorority, Delta Sigma Theta, Sorority Incorporated. "I'm in other states mentoring. I'm in other states helping. It's all about making sure people who look like me have that support. If I can do anything to help them along, I'm going to do that." She is passionate about helping others and finds great joy in her school volunteer work, seeing the smiling children. "That's kind of what keeps me going."

With a soft sigh, Toni said, "I'm a trailblazer, and sometimes I get embarrassed about that. What it's all about is making sure I'm creating a path for others to come behind me and not to have the barriers and deal with some of the issues I had to deal with getting here. The road should definitely be easier for them." This is the focus of her life's work.

She has mentored and encouraged new recruits with these words, "understand there will be barriers and obstacles that will stand in your way. Also, understand there may be a time when you have to take a different path than the path that you originally created but stay on your course. Do not let anybody control your destiny. You know what's yours is yours. Just work hard because nothing comes easy. Know your worth and keep going because if you want it, you can get it, and nobody can stop you." Toni had a career map. Let's explore building one to help you reach your goals.

According to the article "A Roadmap for Career Development: How to Set Your Course," you can build your career in several ways.

- Start by spending time on self-reflection and gathering feedback from others to truly understand your innate strengths, talents, and authentic self-concept.
- Once you have a solid sense of your abilities, define your professional niche or edge—the area where you can offer the most value.
- Examine the gaps between your current competencies and those required for your desired career path. This will allow you to see where you need to develop.
- Develop a five-year plan that maps out how you will gain those missing skills. Remember to account for other life obligations.
- As you execute your plan, remain flexible and adjust based on self-discoveries rather than getting locked into a single rigid outcome.
- Own the management of your career development process, but utilize mentors and advisors like Toni did to provide advice and counsel.
- Frequently pursue opportunities for growth through gaining new skills, taking on projects, and soliciting

feedback to keep making forward progress. Remember that career development is a lifelong process (Munro 2022).

Toni used her roadmap to create success in her career. Without it, she may not have been as successful as she was, but what is career preparation? According to Stringer et al., "Career preparation consists of three dimensions: career decision-making (making a decision about which career to pursue), career planning (using active strategies for achieving career goals), and career confidence (belief in achieving one's career goals)" (2011). Career preparation helps individuals decide which career path to pursue based on their interests, skills, and values. It also allows individuals to develop a roadmap they can follow by reaching milestones and accomplishing goals. Dr. Regina Banks-Hall kept all three dimensions of career planning in mind.

Was she at the right place at the right time, or was it destiny?

Dr. Banks-Hall always knew she was going to be a professor. When she began her position at the sheriff's office, she was working as a contractor when the county decided to privatize the commissary. That decision opened a wonderful opportunity for her. She jumped at the chance to make the organization more efficient.

Unchanged in more than twenty-five years, the commissary at the sheriff's department needed modernizing. Here was her opportunity to impact food service, housekeeping, laundry, and inmate property, all under the umbrella of the commissary. As a seasoned professional at Chrysler and founder of her own company, she would use her expertise to revamp the commissary.

When she began her position as the commissary director, she had already been teaching as an adjunct professor at a university and working on her doctorate. But she knew getting to a full professorship was going to be challenging. "There are a lot of barriers for people of color to get hired into an assistant professor position."

When an opportunity presented itself for her to go on to work at Cleary University as an assistant professor, she took it, but only by doing all the necessary research. That is one thing about Dr. Banks-Hall: Her decisions are made based on much research and with strategy in mind. Working at this new university offered a more direct path to becoming a full-time professor. She left the sheriff's office and accepted the assistant professor position to get in the door and move closer to her ultimate goal.

She believes when strategizing your career, "You have to pay attention, and you've got to seek out your opening, and sometimes you have to take risks. You have to volunteer to do things we may not want to do." It wasn't necessarily about her working at this new university but about the doors that could open faster for her at the new school.

Within one year, a full-time professorship position opened. She asked her boss, "What do I need to do to get that job?" Dr. Banks-Hall completed those tasks, and they promoted her to a full-time professor. There was also a vacant dean position, and the woman selected for the role declined the offer. Within three weeks of becoming a full professor, Dr. Banks-Hall was offered an interim dean's position. Her experience and preparation positioned her to take advantage of these opportunities.

Dr. Banks-Hall attributes her quick promotions to strategy and preparation. She surveyed her environment to find out where there were gaps. She looked around to see what was working and what was not working. She'd noticed a graduate program at the school that no one was paying attention to. What did she do? She made her move and asked to lead that program.

In 2020, after the riots following the death of George Floyd, Dr. Banks-Hall had a conversation with a police officer she taught and helped graduate. During that conversation about police reform, an idea sparked in her head. Whenever you turned on the TV, you'd see much discussion about police reform. In her mind, any police reform would require education.

This became her platform, and she created a degree completion program for law enforcement. Very quickly, her enrollment numbers started increasing, and at least three hundred officers were enrolled in that program. She was working her program and doing what she loved—investing in adults and helping them be successful in their education.

Her experience in two white male-dominated higher education and law enforcement fields has created an interesting perspective. She's seen many women feel they must dumb themselves down to be accepted in an environment or to make people feel comfortable about what they bring. This is particularly true when working with women and women of color. She has developed sound advice for women who want a fulfilling career.

"Women in the public sector and individuals in the public sector have to look for opportunities," said Dr. Banks-Hall. She also believes and tells everyone, "You must be a master in whatever you do. You want mastery, and you want to know your industry forward and backward because you're trying to separate yourself from the competition." Stand out by developing your personal brand, as I discuss in detail in Chapter 9.

## Importance of Career Preparation

According to Dr. Banks-Hall, "You don't have to share your goals with everyone as you're strategizing in your career. Most people you'll be talking to can't help you anyway. What you find is that other folks will squash your dreams." As I like to say, people like that are dream killers. They can't see themselves doing what you want. They find ways to suggest that you cannot accomplish your goals, stand in your way, or worse yet, tell you what you are supposed to do.

Your career is yours. Your dreams and desires are yours, and having individuals around you who are trying to talk you out of what you want to accomplish is not healthy. Some things you need to keep to yourself. When Dr. Banks-Hall wrote her book, she told no one until the book was published. She didn't want to deal with the negative people or the naysayers.

However, sharing your goals with key leaders and decision-makers is essential. You have to understand who the decision-makers are and where the power lies in an organization. Those individuals need to know your desires. For Dr. Banks-Hall, when she told her superiors that she was looking for a full-time job, this ensured they thought of her when a position like that opened up.

Had she not expressed her desire, they may have overlooked her completely. She was always advocating for herself, which is part of preparation. In other words, prepare yourself for opportunities that may open by letting others know your interests.

A challenge for women of color is that they are rarely in positions where they can engage with decision-makers, so you must meet and connect with them intentionally. As a part-time professor, Dr. Banks-Hall taught evening classes, and the administration had gone home by then. She realized if she wanted to meet the administration, she would need to secure a day class, and that is precisely what she did.

It wasn't always easy in these environments that were not welcoming to women of color. "We can't let people make us lose it in the workplace, especially as Black women, because we're going to be labeled angry Black women. We have to fight different types of stereotypes. I just did a workshop yesterday on diversity, equity, and inclusion. I was talking about some of the identities we all bring to the workplace. The stereotype is that for some, for a lot of us, that's not who we are. Because people use a lot of general language to describe you, they automatically label you with that. It's really important to keep that in mind as you're navigating your strategies." In Chapter 6, I provide several stereotypes attributed to Black women.

Dr. Banks-Hall has built a successful thirty-year career through strategic planning and preparation. She has been an executive in the public sector, is currently dean at a university, runs a successful company, and is a best-selling international author. None of her successes are by happenstance. She crafted the business and career she dreamt of through methodical preparation.

Both Toni and Dr. Banks-Hall had no choice but to prepare because of the additional obstacles placed on a woman of color's path. Because of this, career preparation is vital for women of color.

Women of color often face systemic barriers in the job market, including discrimination, bias, stereotyping, and limited access to resources and opportunities. Career preparation can help you develop the skills, knowledge, and networks necessary to overcome these barriers and succeed in your chosen careers. Opportunities will come along, and you must be ready when they do. Preparation is a confidence-building activity that can help you advocate for yourself and the options you wish to explore. Refer to Chapter 3 on building a stronger sense of self. As your career progresses and you are successful, it can help destroy stereotypes about what women of color can achieve. You must be seen in various fields and positions to increase representation, which can lead to greater diversity and inclusion. The next generation needs to see you as you serve as a role model and inspire future generations to dream and pursue their own career goals.

By exploring the three dimensions of career preparation—decision-making, planning, and confidence—we can understand the unique importance of each for women of color, especially those aiming for leadership roles in the public sector. Toni's story highlights how she made her way up the ranks in the fire service through sheer determination and strategic planning. Dr. Banks-Hall's journey adds depth to our understanding of career mapping and emphasizes the power of strategic decision-making and seizing opportunities, even if they come with challenges.

To succeed, preparing and strategically planning for your career is essential. Remember, career mapping is not a luxury. It's a necessity.

# PART II

# OVERCOMING INTERNAL AND EXTERNAL BARRIERS

—

## CHAPTER 5

# REDEFINING FAILURE: HOW PERSONAL SETBACKS CAN PROPEL YOU TO SUCCESS

---

"What if I'm not the superstar I thought I was?"

She entered her student advisor's office one day as an undergrad student at Hampton University in the Airway Science Program. That meeting would send Alyce Hood-Fleming on a trajectory she couldn't have imagined. She had been awaiting the beginning of the pilot training part of the Flight Systems curriculum and stopped in to chat. Her advisor commented that the school was hosting the air traffic exam, and she should take the test to get some job experience. After successfully passing the exam, she was offered a co-op position in Norfolk, Virginia, where she would work during the summers until she graduated from college.

Twenty-one days later, Alyce entered the Air Traffic Academy in Oklahoma City, Oklahoma, and began her career in the specialized and white male-dominated work of an air traffic controller. As a controller, she was responsible for instructing pilots to ensure the pilots maintained separation from one another. She has spent the last thirty-plus years in that career. She has risen from co-op student to Vice President of System Operations, overseeing the National Airspace System operation for the United States.

Like life, success, self-doubt, and a stubbornness to do and say what she believed was right filled her pathway to the top. She spent the first eight years of her career as an en route controller in an old dark building built in 1963 filled with rows of radar scopes. During that time, she held two positions—one as an air traffic controller and the second in the traffic management office.

As she entered her fifth year in traffic management, she realized she needed a change. She thought, *You've been back here too long. You have to recognize when you are not doing your best work. We were out of fresh ideas, and it was time for new eyes.* She accepted a position as a frontline manager (FLM) at Washington Air Route Traffic Control Center (ARTCC) for a year, supervising in an area different than where she worked as a controller.

During that year, she applied for positions in a different district that would give her a broader perspective on air traffic control but was not selected. She couldn't understand what held her back until she met with the district manager. He told her she needed something she didn't have—terminal experience.

"Without the appropriate experience, he said he felt it was a recipe for failure for me and the facility." She understood the logic of that thinking. "The next job you have in the district, in any of your facilities, I'm going to bid on it," stated Alyce.

He responded, "Do you think you can check out?"

Looking him in the eye, Alyce answered, "Absolutely, I will check out." He told her she would return to being a controller, and Alyce responded, "I know. I want the experience and the opportunity to compete." Several bids opened for positions in the district, and she applied and was selected as a supervisor.

Alyce found working as a supervisor in an air traffic control tower one of the most challenging positions. As an en route controller, she was accustomed to looking at a radar scope, but she had to look out the window in the tower to see the planes. She needed to learn all the positions to better assist her employees as a supervisor. Although she felt proud of herself for stepping out of her comfort zone, she was more comfortable in the tower than she used to be in the en route environment.

This experience made Alyce question her skills as a controller, but after successfully certifying and supervising in that environment, she got the chance to work in a different position. This field often requires moving around and working in various facilities.

When she was selected for a position at one of her previous facilities, an act of God allowed her to excel. On October 12, 2012, Hurricane Sandy slammed into the East Coast of the US and crippled the NY and New Jersey area. From her role at the Command Center, Alyce shined. "I managed a lot of those hurricane calls, and that's when the VP of System Ops knew who I was." Again, Alyce successfully bid and secured a new position. This time, a "great recommendation from that VP" would help close the deal.

Given her past positive working relationships, Alyce expected the employees to welcome her as the new air traffic manager. "It was interesting because having been a supervisor there, I came back expecting the same level of love that I had gotten there as air traffic manager, but it was a different environment." One of the biggest hurdles she faced was that one of the managers in the facility had also competed for the job and was unhappy that Alyce got it instead. This created tension in the facility.

Alyce handled the tension by focusing on the rules. "I literally live in the rules and regs," so if it's in black and white, then "that's what it is." Alyce's management style worsened the situation by hammering employees over the head with the rules and causing swirls in the facility. "One thing I had to learn was to understand the areas of gray. It took me a long time to understand that you can be right every single time and really lose that battle."

The challenges she faced caused her to question her abilities. "In this role, for the first time, I realized I might not be successful in something I tried. Not that I was always successful in everything, but I had not failed, and so I faced failure for the first time." If something didn't change, she would not survive the environment. It wasn't something that changed. It was someone that came along—a mentor. "I'm going to tell you I believe that he saved my career. I don't think there's any question that he gave me some advice that I didn't want to take, but I did. I listened."

She hadn't asked for help, but for some reason, he saw what was happening and decided to step in and help her. She didn't understand why the situation was getting worse. Unfortunately, Alyce had gotten locked into being right, and that was coming out in her engagements. "It was interesting because I kept asking, 'What am I doing wrong? What did I do that was against the regulations that was wrong?'" What her mentor told her was an important lesson and critical for success as a leader. He said, "You have to talk to people. You can't just say it. You can't just proclaim it even if the regs say it. That's not the environment we work in."

After receiving advice from her mentor, she followed it. He also recommended her for a new temporary position, which she was selected for. However, she was pulled out of the position prematurely, leading to her frustration and anger. "I was devastated, to be perfectly honest, because I thought I was just getting my feet. I was starting to feel comfortable in the role, and then they said, 'No, thank you. We don't need you anymore.'"

After that disappointment, her mentor gave her direct feedback on how her actions and decisions impacted the people who worked for her and how they affected her career. He suggested that she not return to her air traffic manager position and take another role, such as the executive and technical representative, to help her develop different people skills.

"It is the best thing that could ever have happened to me because I learned so much about how to manage, how to collaborate, and how to work not just with colleagues but with the union and how to look at situations in a different way. Why are you so spooled up about two minutes? All those kinds of things. It was the best job I ever had because it advanced my learning in a way that I don't think going back as the air traffic manager could have done. I think going back would have been it for my career path because I was still really disappointed. I was a little bit angry. I was sad. I was embarrassed. You know, all the things that you feel when you feel like you've been fired."

Though Alyce is a woman of strong conviction and believes in herself and her abilities, she chooses to listen to her mentor, and it takes a lot of talking on his part because she is "stubborn." He didn't have to help her. "But he did. He had nothing to gain from helping me. He just decided that he saw something in me, and he wanted to see me be successful."

## Resilience and Mindset

What Alyce learned was success comes with setbacks. Career setbacks are disappointing and can cause feelings of hopelessness. It is not the challenge or the obstacle that is the problem but how you handle it. Your mindset will determine how you recover. If you reframe the setback as a learning opportunity, you can recover with more significant mental strength and clarity to develop a plan and move forward.

The recovery is known as career resilience or CR. In an empirical literature review, Mishra and McDonald define CR as a "developmental process of persisting, adapting, and/ or flourishing in one's career despite challenges, changing events, and disruptions over time" (2017). This definition recognizes impacts over the length of a career, that it is not a singular process, and that the environment and personal life impact a person's resilience (2017). This suggests that resilience can change and grow.

In the article, "The Resilience Mindset: Cultivating Inner Strength for Life's Ups and Downs," having a resilient mindset is crucial to adapting to unexpected situations. Key characteristics include optimism, adaptability, and emotional regulation. A growth mindset is a key component, encouraging individuals to view challenges as opportunities for growth. Your mindset is the foundation for building resilience (Sargent 2023).

Much like Alyce, I, too, faced a career setback. An unexpected setback came after many successes, but I had to face it.

Maybe I had made a mistake accepting this new position.

I felt a mix of excitement and fear when I learned I had been chosen for a second-level manager position. Although I didn't have much subject matter expertise in the organization, I was eager to take on the challenge. My selection was unexpected, both to me and others, mainly because I had just been enrolled in an executive leadership development program and had assumed that would be my focus for the following year.

However, the director of our organization had a different plan for me. He told me he believed I was the right person to step into that role. I had been experiencing the joy that comes from recent success. In eighteen months, I moved to a new state, built a new team, and successfully met our goals. My confidence was at an all-time high, so I jumped at the opportunity for a new position and personal growth.

That joy would end quickly. The management team doubted me from the start because they didn't know me and knew I did not have their background. I also faced direct hostility from one of the managers who reported to me. Well, I thought I had it all figured out. I like to build relationships and connect as humans, so I reached into my metaphorical tool belt and repeated how I had historically built relationships. It didn't work.

I had built relationships by getting to know individuals and connecting with them where we had commonalities. It wasn't going to work because the manager who had the hostility wanted the job that I was in, and she was unhappy. I felt like she didn't believe I should be there. I found her remarkably unhelpful and nasty in her engagements with me. If I asked her anything, she frowned, looked at me, and would answer me with the fewest words possible.

I still didn't want to give up because I believed I could somehow make this woman see me and recognize that I only wanted to be supportive and for us to have a collaborative team and to do great work. But nothing I tried worked. For example, I secured some leadership training to come in and help us learn about each other and how we can work together. That didn't work. She participated, but her responses were generic and not personal. During one-on-one meetings, I shared a little bit about myself in the hopes that she would share a little bit about herself, but that didn't work, either. Nothing I knew to do was working, and I was perplexed.

After several months had gone by, nothing changed.

Another challenge presented itself. The director I worked for previously worked with this manager. They had an excellent professional relationship, and he rendered me completely powerless, whether he knew it or not. She didn't think she had to work with me. She thought she could go around me and go to him to get things done. It was a miserable situation, and I remember sleepless Sunday nights because I didn't want to face Monday.

The crippling doubt was rearing its head with frequent headaches. I questioned myself and whether I should have taken that promotion. Whether I had the right skill sets to learn this work and connect with the managers to build a team, in my mind, we couldn't be successful if you had one of the leaders on that team actively pulling against you. I was at my wits' end.

Finally, I understood that it didn't matter what I tried. Nothing would change if she was unwilling to do something very different. I couldn't change her, but I could communicate the issues with my manager and see if we could address the second challenge.

I told him very directly that his engagement was causing problems. That somehow, this manager didn't believe I was her supervisor and that she had to work with me and go through me. I further told him that if he wanted to keep working directly with her, maybe I wasn't the leader he needed in this organization.

I have to give him credit. He received the feedback well and agreed with me. He stopped allowing her to circumvent me, meaning she and I would at least discuss getting the work done. For the first time, it felt like a supervisor-to-employee relationship. However, we had no engagement beyond that.

Things stayed that way for the following year. No magic pill improved everything, and suddenly, we had this excellent relationship. That manager decided to take another opportunity for which she was very skilled. Her absence changed the dynamic of our team, and we experienced greater cohesion.

The funny thing is that, as life would have it, I later had the opportunity to work with her again. I don't know if it was just the passage of time or just getting to know each other on the periphery, but somehow, that negative energy had dissipated, and whatever was standing in the middle of us was no longer there. We were able to have a professional relationship. We may have reached a place with a level of professional respect.

I offer this because I don't care how remarkable your career is. A time will come when you're going to face something that causes you to question yourself, and you'll realize there's nothing you can do. I had never experienced a situation I could not figure out. You can figure out anything. However, even with a resilient mindset, human relations was one thing I couldn't overcome.

## How to Overcome Setbacks

For women of color, CR is essential for a variety of reasons. We often face systemic barriers, microaggressions, and discriminatory workplace practices, making it challenging to achieve career success. Our setbacks are more complicated because when one of us fails, it is generalized to all women of color, thus making it difficult for other women.

CR is a process that can be developed. Here are some steps.

- Accept the discomfort. I had to accept that things were what they were no matter what I tried to do.
- Focus on the only thing you can control, which is you. The only thing I could control was my actions. I showed up daily as a professional despite what I was feeling inside. I continued treating her respectfully and professionally, never altering how I engaged with her.
- Evaluate the situation to determine what went wrong. It's vital to understand your role in what happened so you don't repeat the behavior.
- Rely on the network you have built, whether it is family, friends, or colleagues. Seek out their support and seek honest feedback from them. They will have insights that could be helpful. According to Riggio, our close friends better understand our behavior since they can provide an objective viewpoint, offer a unique perspective,

and attribute our actions to our character rather than situational factors (2016).

- Develop a growth mindset. That means you believe you can learn and develop new skills. Look for learning opportunities that support your career goals. Alyce's story showed that while a side-step position didn't progress her in that moment, it did benefit her in the long run. Sometimes, you have to move laterally to move up eventually.
- Review your current goals. Are they still applicable? Do you need to explore other career options and possibly develop new goals?

Alyce and I experienced self-doubt and workplace tension but found resilience crucial for success. We learned that following the rules isn't always enough, and in some instances, nothing you try will work. Effective leadership requires adaptability and emotional intelligence. Through our resilient mindset, we overcame setbacks and evolved, offering valuable lessons for career resilience.

## CHAPTER 6

# SHATTERING STEREOTYPES: TRIUMPHING OVER RACISM AND BIAS

———

"You are not the typical young Black person."

Talethia responded, "What does that mean?"

Her boss replied, "You are twenty-five, you have a condo, you are on the rise. That's not typical."

When her boss made that comment, Talethia did not know what to feel or think about the comment. His comments were microaggressions, but Talethia did not know that. She didn't recognize the comments as discriminatory. She realized retrospectively, "She didn't know what she didn't know."

After graduating from a predominately white institution, Talethia Thomas began her public service career as an intern for the Department of the Army. She did not experience race and gender discrimination until she began working. Her career started with two other female interns. Her boss, a high-ranking federal government employee, reluctantly accepted the interns. He treated them not as interns but as administrative staff, refusing to allow them to experience the full benefits of the intern program, like mentorship and rotational assignments. A recent Gallup poll found that about 23 percent of Black women experience workplace discrimination (Lloyd 2021).

Talethia recounts that when the military generals would visit their office, her manager would ask the interns to make coffee. Talethia, a self-appointed, sassy, outspoken woman, responded, "I don't like coffee. I don't drink coffee, and I am not making coffee." She refused.

The experience represented what it felt to work for that manager. Talethia never reported her boss's behavior. Instead, she fought back the only way she knew—by speaking up and questioning him directly. She worked in this environment for several years, and when a new wave of interns arrived, someone documented and reported the discriminatory behavior.

The next position she held placed her in another male-dominated work environment at the Department of Treasury on a financial audit team. One of her responsibilities included auditing the inventories of seized assets. Appointed as the auditor in charge, she traveled to the central US to audit a law enforcement organization in a predominately white environment. Surprise greeted her upon her arrival. They did not expect to see a young Black female auditor leading the team. They dismissed her and failed to cooperate with her requests. She felt uncomfortable. She stepped into another room and took a moment, gathering herself.

A quick call to her manager refocused her and empowered her to finish the job, but not before a quick stop in the bathroom.

"I took a deep breath and literally talked to myself as I looked in the mirror. I had to tell myself: you're where you're supposed to be. You belong. You know what you're doing. You need to go out there and handle your business. This is your job, and you need to do it." Mustering confidence, she returned to the room and restarted the audit.

With clarity, she firmly provided direction and clear expectations. They tried to deviate from the process, but she refused to allow it. "I understood the assignment. I knew what I needed to do, and midway through the audit, I was my authentic self, just smiling and talking." By the end of the day, they worked well together. They offered her tickets to a baseball game and treated her respectfully for the remainder of the audit in a relaxed work environment. The experience taught her the importance of staying true to herself and acknowledging that she was where she belonged no matter how uncomfortable the situation. She now knows what it takes to accomplish the task.

Working across multiple federal agencies in her twenty-five-year career, Talethia overcame inappropriate comments, dismissive treatment, and hostility from her male colleagues. Her treatment stemmed from the stereotypical lens that many see "Black" women. Relying on her self-awareness, knowing her value, and willingness to learn enabled her to thrive despite challenges reaching the senior executive service in the federal government. She emerged more empowered, advocating for other women of color to know they belong and must use their voices. She serves as an inspiration for overcoming stereotypes and adversity through self-belief.

## Stereotypes Defined

Talethia faced stereotyping based on her ethnicity and her gender. This stereotyping is referred to as intersectionality. Intersectionality considers how multiple marginalized identities, like gender and race, intersect and result in unique experiences of discrimination (Wong 2022).

Gender stereotypes are oversimplified beliefs about individuals or groups based on their gender. Media, advertising, and socialization often perpetuate these beliefs. They can hurt people's opportunities, choices, and self-expression. For instance, common gender stereotypes include men being aggressive and unemotional while women are nurturing and emotional. Such beliefs can lead to discrimination, prejudice, and social inequality while contributing to gender-based violence.

Ethnic stereotypes, based on cultural or racial differences, on the other hand, are negative beliefs about a particular ethnic group. These stereotypes can also lead to discrimination and prejudice, harming individuals and entire communities. Examples of ethnic stereotypes include the idea that certain groups are lazy, criminal, or unintelligent. Challenging and debunking such stereotypes is essential, as they can perpetuate systemic racism and discrimination.

Black women in America face a range of stereotypes. They "are routinely defined by a specific set of grotesque caricatures that are reductive, inaccurate, and unfair" (Jones and Shorter-Gooden 2004, 3). Some common stereotypes include:

1. The "strong Black woman" stereotype portrays Black women as unbreakable and able to handle anything. It ignores the reality of mental health and the need for

support. While it may seem optimistic, it can also lead to unrealistic expectations and prevent Black women from seeking help when needed (Jones and Shorter-Gooden 2004, 18-22).

2. The "unprofessional" stereotype portrays Black women as unprofessional, uneducated, or lacking in qualifications used to justify discriminatory hiring practices or unequal pay.

3. The "over-sexualized" stereotype portrays Black women as hyper-sexualized and promiscuous. Commonly referred to as "Jezebel," it is rooted in the history of slavery and sexual exploitation of Black women and is used to justify sexual harassment and assault (Jones and Shorter-Gooden 2004, 29-32; Harris-Perry 2011, 33-35).

4. The "mammy" stereotype portrays Black women as nurturing, self-sacrificing, and always putting the needs of others before their own. The image was born out of slavery, where "she was the loyal, hard-working, caring, and trustworthy slave who was the chief caretaker of the plantation's master and his family (Smith and Nkomo 2021, 245). This negatively impacts Black women because the perception is that they care for everyone, which clouds their other professional gifts (Smith and Nkomo 2021, 245).

5. The "sapphire" stereotype, also called "angry Black woman," portrays Black women as aggressive, hostile, and easily angered. It is an excuse to dismiss or discredit their opinions and emotions. As Harris-Perry (2011) states in her book *Sister Citizen Shame, Stereotypes, and Black Women in America*, "This stereotype does not acknowledge Black women's anger as a legitimate reaction to unequal circumstances. It is seen as a pathological, irrational desire to control Black men, families, and communities" (95).

Kris, a Black female law enforcement officer, stepped in and gave a simple direction in the chaos of an overflowing toilet, spilling feces onto the floor. "Hey, let us regroup, get your PPE, and put on your eye protection."

A lieutenant at the time, she responded to help other officers with an inmate flooding the ward floor. It was a stressful moment. With an elevated and forceful voice, a subordinate white male officer responded, "You don't even know what we are going through here."

His response assumed that she didn't have the background to hold the rank on her sleeves. "As a Black female law enforcement supervisor, you constantly must deal with the stereotype of how you got your position, whether you are qualified for the job, or your direction is questioned. If I was a white woman, I don't feel like he would have done that to me. In that job as a Black female, you feel very unprotected."

These types of engagements were common in her work environment, yet they did not hinder her from attaining the position of Commander. Overcoming stereotypes based on gender and the strong Black woman trope filled her career path. "You don't get the help, mental support, or anything that you need from anybody. They just expect you to make a way. You can't have a weak moment in there. If you do, you are viewed as less than, like you can't supervise or you can't handle it. You really must hide all of that from people. To them, that trope means you don't need anything." Also, in the environment, they believe the stereotype that Black women are unmarried, so they don't believe you have the support of a spouse or partner.

A commonly held belief in law enforcement is that women who get ahead only do so because they are sleeping around. This pervasive belief makes Kris guard her engagement with colleagues. She describes herself as a happy-go-lucky person who likes to joke around, but at work, she can't do that for fear of accusations of being called a whore.

"I must compartmentalize. If you let your guard down in that place, suddenly it's 'She's messing around with someone.' It's so bad that you can't even go to lunch with a guy, even a partner." The men at work regularly go to lunch, meet after work, and golf together. She rarely participates, remaining cautious about putting herself in a position for people to gossip about her.

There's always isolation as a female in the environment, and her decision to separate herself had no impact on her career. Kris had her core group of work friends and focused on those relationships. They became part of her support system, helping her cope with the environment.

She doesn't believe she overcame the stereotyping, but she developed coping mechanisms to survive the toxic environment. She credits the champions supporting her career, professional and external networks, and supportive family and friends. "I will say I worked hard and did not complain at work even though I would go home and drag them for filth to my spouse."

"I didn't openly complain about some of the things I thought didn't make sense to me. I just did it to the best of my ability. Another thing I will say is if I didn't like it, I found a way not to do it." Senior officers often gave women menial tasks, administrative, or busy work. "I didn't do it. I just said okay, and then I wouldn't do it."

Instead, what she learned was the business of law enforcement. Two champions played roles in her career. Both individuals had jobs in another law enforcement agency before joining the office where she worked. One individual was a Black male, and the other was a Black female. They were both ranked highly in her department. The male was instrumental in her selection into a powerful supervisor position that gave her organizational and public visibility.

In that position, "I learned to do budgets, negotiate contracts, and staffing." The expertise she developed helped cement her promotion to commander. When the commander position became vacant, the Black female put her name into the conversation. "You have to have a sponsor. Somebody in that space believes you can do it and will mention your name and put in the good word because, in our environment, you can't do it by yourself."

She faced constant challenges to her qualifications and authority but rose to commander through hard work, mentorship, and a willingness to adapt. She navigated a toxic work environment filled with gender and race stereotypes by developing coping mechanisms such as compartmentalizing emotions and avoiding gossip. Kris's story highlights that stereotypes don't have to limit one's potential if they persist. Let's explore how to overcome the limitations.

## Navigating Stereotypes

Talethia and Kris used similar strategies to navigate the environment. Both women relentlessly focused on their objectives, refusing to allow stereotyping to hinder their progress. They excelled in their roles. It wasn't that they believed they overcame the stereotypes, but they learned to navigate successfully. There are intentional approaches for excelling despite the environment.

For Black women such as Talethia and Kris, overcoming stereotypes requires a combination of education, awareness, and positive representation. Here are some strategies people may use to overcome stereotypes:

1. Educating oneself and others about Black people's history, culture, and traditions can help challenge and dispel negative stereotypes and misconceptions.

2. Showcasing positive representations of Black people in media, arts, and other forms of popular culture can help counteract negative stereotypes and highlight the diversity and richness of Black culture.

3. Celebrating and preserving language, traditions, and arts can help reinforce positive cultural identities and counteract negative stereotypes and misconceptions. For Black people, this requires learning about your history preslavery and tracing roots back to your country of origin in Africa.

4. Engaging in open and honest dialogue with individuals and groups with prejudiced attitudes can help challenge and dismantle these attitudes over time. Research shows positive group contact reduces prejudice and improves intergroup relations (Eberhardt and Tropp 2021).

5. Building a strong sense of community and working together to address stereotypes and misconceptions can be a powerful tool. This includes organizing events, workshops, and other initiatives to promote positive cultural identity.

6. Being true to yourself and your values, which I cover in "Hair, Identity, and Power: Owning Your True Self at Work." Like Kris, if the job is something an admin assistant can do, don't do it, and remind your coworker

that it isn't your job. Katrina demonstrated the same behavior in the chapter on Hair, Identity, and Power.

7. Researchers conducted two studies to determine if positive affirmations helped women when dealing with the threat of stereotyping, one involving a difficult math test and another involving a spatial rotation test. They found that women engaging in positive affirmations performed significantly better in both trials, effectively neutralizing the adverse effects. Self-affirmation did not impact men's scores on the spatial rotation test (Martens 2006, 236-243).

8. Look for positive role models and groups to find your support network. This could be work-related, faith-related, or a social club. See Chapter 10 on networking for more.

9. Research suggests finding ways to emphasize similarities and shared identities could help counter divisiveness (Craig-Henderson 2020).

10. Mental health and self-care are essential. Seek help if you need it.

## Overcoming Implicit Bias

Implicit bias is unconscious attitudes or stereotypes that affect our actions and decisions. An essential first step is recognizing that everyone has implicit biases that can negatively impact interactions and outcomes. Each person should accept responsibility for identifying and understanding their own implicit biases.

To work effectively with colleagues, individuals can use techniques like replacing stereotypes with nonstereotypical thinking, practicing perspective-taking to understand different viewpoints, building interpersonal contacts across groups, regulating emotional reactions, and adopting mindfulness. By consistently using these strategies, individuals can develop a habit of nonbiased thinking, which can help reduce stereotyping in their interactions at work. The key is acknowledging implicit biases and actively using techniques like perspective-taking and mindfulness to minimize biased behaviors and decisions when working with colleagues (Health and Human Services, n.d.).

Gender and racial stereotyping are pervasive, creating unique barriers for women of color where they intersect. Nevertheless, the stories of Talethia and Commander Kris demonstrate how resilience, mentorship, and an unshakeable sense of purpose can help individuals thrive despite discrimination.

We all must take responsibility for recognizing our biases, using techniques like perspective-taking to overcome them, and creating workplaces of diversity, equity, inclusion, and belonging. Though the struggle continues, we can gradually dismantle the oppressive stereotypes that limit human potential through open dialogue, education, and positive representation.

## CHAPTER 7

# FROM TARGET TO VICTOR: OVERCOMING HOSTILITY

———

The white female cashier had been pleasant and helpful to the customer in front of Marisol. After she rang up Marisol Craig's items, she asked, "Do you have a card?"

Perplexed, "I was like, what?"

The cashier responded, "Do you have an EBT card? Where's your card?"

Marisol answered, "I don't understand what you are asking me."

The cashier said, "How are you paying for this?"

Dr. Marisol Craig was furious. She realized the cashier had just stereotyped her, and Marisol attributed that experience to the cashier seeing that she had mixed-race children. That experience was an "aha moment" for her. As a fairer-skinned Latina, she had never experienced anything like that and was close to fifty years old.

"I never really understood some of the issues my sisters who have darker skin faced. They would call me the white girl of the family. That's why you've never experienced anything. People think you're white. And I never really understood what that meant."

Dr. Craig grew up in Reading, Pennsylvania, in a predominately Hispanic community. There were no teachers of color in her formative years, nor did she have any in college. She didn't have any role models in education who looked like her. There was no representation, which was one of the reasons Marisol wanted to teach.

"I'm still the only Latina administrator in my district in the last twenty years, even with a growing Latino population in our districts. When I started, it was approximately 11 percent, and now we're at 20 or 32 percent."

When Marisol started teaching, she focused on the children and doing excellent work. Unknown to her, an influential white male superintendent from another district recognized her talents and then recruited her to his district. "He just really loved my energy. He loved my passion. He loved the perspectives I had to bring coming from another district with different things." She accepted an amazing opportunity. However, her peers did not welcome her into the district.

Seen as an outsider, her colleagues were apprehensive about working with her. This didn't stop her, though, because within twenty-four months, she received two promotions, landing her in an administrative role. "I was a very young administrator." Those two quickly earned promotions furthered the divide between Marisol and her colleagues. The rumor mill was abuzz about how she rapidly climbed the ladder.

"Other people who had been waiting and working their way up and, I guess, trying to get into position, so I dealt with a lot of: 'She's the golden child. She must be sleeping with him. She's flipping on people and snitching, and that's how she got her job.'" It was a challenging time for Marisol. She was a young administrator of about twenty-seven years old and did not have the experience to deal with the turmoil. She did what she knew to show up and prove she was worthy of the position. At this point, an important mentor, Walter, entered her life.

Walter, a Latino man in administration in her district, saw her struggles, and he stepped in to help her through them. "You have to get past all this. You have to really show them that you know what you're doing." He advised her on handling the politics and moving past the conspiracy theories surrounding her promotions. "He just walked and talked me through, and he really modeled a lot of things for me, like how to have tough conversations with people, how to collect documentation around people, how to set up programs, and how to give people feedback. I just didn't know how to have those conversations because I'd never had them before." One key lesson he taught her was the importance of holding people accountable.

She would practice what she learned from him throughout her career. "I remember him saying, 'There's not a lot of us here. You have to really step it up and know what you're doing 110 percent. Make sure people respect you.' It took me a little bit to really prove to people that I knew what I was doing and that I was a genuine person."

It finally happened. They got to experience the real Marisol. One of her colleagues told her, "We were told you were a snake, and we didn't like you. After getting to know you, you are the complete opposite."

Walter left his position, and Maria stepped into his role. It was not as joyous an experience as she would have hoped. The district was looking for a change from Walter, and they did not get it with Marisol. He had mentored her and helped her see what good administration looks like, and she had adapted what she learned to fit her style. His influence was apparent in the way she conducted business. She continued to excel in her career and deal with the labels colleagues would place on her.

As the only Latina, Marisol has dealt with stereotypes in her career. She recounted attending a meeting on behalf of her boss, the district superintendent. As she walked into the meeting, she introduced herself as the assistant superintendent and stated that she was representing her boss because of a scheduling conflict. A man and woman began to speak to her as if she were his secretary or personal assistant.

"Well, can you tell him this," they said.

"No, I think you're misunderstanding," I said. "I'm not his secretary."

It was another example of the stereotyping that she dealt with. After Marisol explained, they understood her position. They couldn't imagine she had a senior role leading the seven-thousand-student district. "People don't really see me as the second in charge in the district."

Because she is a woman, she has been unfairly typecast as complacent and discouraged from advocating for herself. During one of her past performance discussions, Marisol had to represent herself. The school district is under a court-appointed receivership, and the organization's supervisor is outside of the school district and is court-appointed.

The supervisor is responsible for the performance of the superintendent and the assistant superintendent. She cited things in Marisol's performance evaluation that Marisol disagreed with. Craig sat in disbelief for several minutes, thinking, *You shouldn't have a third party giving you information about my performance.* The supervisor was regurgitating what others had told her about Marisol, showing favoritism as if it were fact.

Marisol was not going to accept what was being said about her silently. She had earned her position and the right to speak her mind. She had learned to advocate for herself initially from her mother, a very independent woman who told her to get educated, and from years of observing things she didn't think were right. She remained silent earlier for fear that it would impact her career. "I saw what happened to people who spoke out. They were targeted. I've seen people quit work because of their health. It was so stressful."

In a calm voice, Marisol says, "Excuse me. I'm so sorry. Can I stop you? Can we go back to this point? Can I respond?"

The supervisor said, "Of course."

Marisol says, "First of all, I'm really offended with this piece because you have no evidence of this. This is all hearsay, and I'd really like to understand better or more about how you came to this conclusion."

The supervisor's eyebrows raised, and her eyes widened. "It came to my attention that you're demonstrating favoritism among staff members."

Marisol maintained her composure, "I said, 'Really? So, what does that mean?'"

The response was, "People see you, and I know you've been here for a while. You have relationships."

Marisol knew what that meant. "What I'm hearing you say is that it's about what white people feel. My white supervisor feels I show people of color favoritism."

Marisol was shocked. "I help whoever asked for help. I can't help if they come to me, and I can't help if people visually see that it happens to be a Black teacher or a Latino teacher, or whatever. I don't go around saying to my white colleagues, you have favoritism because you hang around all white people. It's just a natural thing, right." The supervisor was dumbfounded, and Marisol didn't stop there. "It's perception. And you should not be led by perception. You should really ask deeper questions."

They went back and forth on a few other topics until something changed. Eventually, the supervisor said something unexpected. Marisol explained, "The supervisor said, 'You know what? You're being very adversarial with me right now. It's almost borderline disrespectful, and I'm feeling uncomfortable right now. I did not expect this from you.'" Marisol was angry, but she maintained her cool.

After she went home and calmed down, Marisol told her husband. "The audacity for her to say that to me, I wasn't yelling. Then I had to start thinking, wow, because my husband talks about this a lot as a Black man. I was like, wow, if I had been darker skinned, that could have gone even worse. They expect me not to come back at them or respond to something I disagree with, just being complacent. I now realize, as I got older, that being light-skinned did help me in a lot of ways. I guess people see me as less threatening, for whatever reason, because we know that's a huge stereotype."

Marisol remained calm throughout the gossip, rumors, and spreading lies about her. She experienced treatment she didn't expect, rose above it, and continued to be successful.

## Hostilities Defined

Workplace hostility for women of color refers to any form of mistreatment, discrimination, or harassment that women of color experience due to their race, ethnicity, and gender. This can include but is not limited to being subject to verbal harassment, being excluded from important opportunities, being unfairly evaluated, being threatened, being passed over for promotions, or being paid less than their colleagues with similar qualifications and experience.

Workplace hostility can also include microaggressions, which are subtle and often unintentional acts that communicate negative stereotypes about people of color, such as what Dr. Craig faced after her promotion. These can include comments or behaviors that make assumptions about an individual's ability, intelligence, or cultural identity and can damage a person's self-esteem and sense of belonging in the workplace.

Workplace hostility, especially for women of color, can significantly impact their well-being, career advancement, and overall job satisfaction. Organizations have a responsibility to create a culture that is inclusive, supportive, and respectful of all employees, regardless of their race, ethnicity, or gender, to create a productive and healthy work environment. This includes political organizations and those elected to public office. Those women of color elected may face more hostility because the First Amendment protects free speech and the belief of some people that politicians are public property rather than individuals.

According to a June 29, 2021, PBS news report entitled, "For Black Women in Government, Highlighting Threats and Abuse Can Make It Worse," Black women at the highest political offices in the country experience hostility, intimidation, racism, sexism, and regular death threats. Their problems extend beyond the usual political battles. Interviews with eighteen women reveal that nearly all of them have dealt with some form of abuse, with many receiving death threats. Despite the dangers, these women are motivated to stay in office to prove that the abuse will not silence them. However, some note they have limits and would leave office if the danger becomes too severe. The women feel connected to the constituents they represent and champion issues related to the Black community (Nawaz).

Schaeffer states, "Women of color have served in Congress for almost six decades" (2023). Of the 423 women elected to Congress, 106 have been women of color, and most have been elected within the last ten years (2023). Even after sixty years of service, the system often lacks support to address the issues and protect these women from harassment. Here are some examples of the challenges specific women politicians face, mentioned in the June 17, 2021, PBS news report entitled, "More Black Women Are Being Elected to Office. Few Feel Safe Once They Get There":

- Kiah Morris faced years of harassment and threats, even after moving to a new city. Her young son built a "panic room" in their home to feel safe. Morris eventually resigned from office in 2018 due to the threats.
- The Baltimore State's Attorney, Marilyn Mosby, received violently racist voicemail messages filled with expletives and slurs.
- Multiple women like Jahana Hayes and Nikema Williams received frequent death threats and were concerned about shootings targeting Black politicians.
- Attica Scott always thinks about escape routes if someone tries to shoot Black people in the Capitol building. She feels she can't express herself freely like white male politicians.

- Shirley Weber feels pressure to represent the entire Black community and community expectations to succeed as one of few Black women politicians.
- Candice Norwood said some women were reluctant to speak to the media about the harassment because it often leads to increased attacks afterward.

These women find little refuge in the law, and existing laws offer limited protections, with unclear boundaries between free speech and harassment. Though some women pay for personal security, most lack resources or institutional support. Still, brave Black women enter politics, demanding change despite grave risks.

Nikema Williams and others now live in constant fear, requiring security details. The path forward remains perilous, yet their tenacity inspires future leaders. By boldly condemning injustice, even at significant personal cost, these courageous women are creating a more just and equitable society for all (Norwood, Jones, and Bolaji 2021).

To create a more just and equitable society for all, it's essential to recognize the obstacles that women of color face in politics and the workplace. Hostility and discrimination can be just as prevalent in the professional sphere, making it difficult for women of color to thrive and succeed.

## Overcoming Hostilities

A qualitative literature review conducted by Dhanraj Shardhana to determine the impact of workplace hostilities on employees' work-life balance suggests several ways that organizations can combat hostility:

- Implement strict policies against harassment and discrimination with accountability measures to provide a sense of security for employees. Taking action against offenders can build a culture of respect.
- When organizations respond quickly to offenses and hold perpetrators responsible, it demonstrates a commitment to ensuring a healthy, safe workplace.
- Taking appropriate action against offenders who engage in hostile behaviors like bullying, harassment, or discrimination can contribute to building a workplace culture of respect and fairness.
- Holding individuals responsible for unethical, hostile conduct signals that such behaviors will not be tolerated and can deter future incidents.
- Accountability promotes adherence to anti-harassment and anti-discrimination policies by showing that violations will incur consequences (2023).

If you encounter or witness hostility:

- Utilize employee resources such as diversity and inclusion programs, employee assistance programs, and other support services available through the organization.
- Document any incidents of hostility or discrimination that you experience in the workplace. Keep a record of the incident's date, time, and details as well as any witnesses who can corroborate your account.
- Seek legal advice if you believe you have been the victim of discrimination or harassment. Contact an attorney or your organization's human resources department to explore your options.

- Like Dr. Craig, remain calm and use your voice to call out unacceptable behavior.
- If you are an ally, do not sit quietly on the sideline watching the behavior. Use your voice to address it.
- This behavior toward our elected officials is egregious. We need other elected officials and constituents to support our politicians by calling out unacceptable behavior and holding offenders accountable.

The path toward justice requires courage. Dr. Marisol Craig and the brave Black women politicians demonstrated tenacity and resilience despite hostility. They remained committed to their communities and stood as pillars of strength.

Their actions inspire our engagement. As citizens, we must speak out against harassment of public officials and demand accountability. As organizations, we must implement policies that foster inclusion. As individuals, we must check our own biases.

Most importantly, we must empower the next generation of women of color to lead. Together, we can build a society of mutual understanding and respect. Do not stay silent. Speak out against intolerance. Support victims and hold offenders accountable. Through solidarity, empathy, and moral courage, we can overcome hostility. Our collective voice is powerful.

# CHAPTER 8

# BOUNCING BACK: THE POWER OF GRIT AND RESILIENCE

---

Tiffany stopped midstep and stood there as two women walked past her, and she counted the five stripes on the shoulder of one of the women's dress uniforms. She had never seen that many stripes on a woman and certainly not an African American female.

After the initial surprise turned to curiosity, Tiffany ran down the hall behind the women and tapped one of them on the shoulder. The woman's head spun around like the infamous *Exorcist* scene, or at least that's how she remembered it. She chuckled while telling the story. The woman turned around, saying, "How can I help you?"

"Are you a chief?" Tiffany asked with childlike wonder.

With confidence and poise, Chief Rosemary Cloud answered, "Of course I am."

"I have never seen a Black female fire chief," said Tiffany.

Chief Cloud responded, "Because I am the first and won't be the last."

Tiffany looked at the woman standing next to her. Counting to herself: one, two, three, four, stripes, Tiffany realized that the woman was high ranking and was right up under the Chief.

"Let's stay in touch. This is my assistant, Toni Washington, and she will give you my contact information," the Chief said. Tiffany did not stay in touch with Chief Cloud, but this began a friendship with Assistant Chief Washington.

This brief exchange convinced Tiffany that she could do her job in the fire service. She had no intentions of seeking a promotion. She wanted to excel at her work and provide for her daughter.

Tiffany grew up and received her education in Prince George's County, Maryland, which held the title of the most affluent Black County in the US until recently. She actively participated in both academics and athletics during high school, excelling in both.

She followed a traditional path, entering college at George Washington University to become a doctor. One of her electives was emergency medical technician (EMT), which required her to ride along at a fire station. She recalled telling her mom that she didn't know the location of the fire station. It was a neighborhood fire station, and her mother found it "crazy" that Tiffany didn't know it existed.

She completed a few weeks of ride-alongs and enjoyed the work. She volunteered in the fire service while finishing her degree and subsequently accepted a position with the federal government. After a few years of following the traditional career path, Tiffany did not find her day-to-day job as rewarding as her volunteer work. She wanted to give back to the community through public safety and enjoyed helping people daily. She decided to enter the fire department as a recruit.

Entering her class of about 120, it was apparent that the field was male-dominated. The course had a maximum of twelve women. Very few were people of color. The classwork was demanding, requiring physical strength and mental toughness. There were no concessions for women, and Tiffany sometimes felt that the instructors intentionally made the work more difficult for women.

The real challenge for women became apparent in recruiting school. Tiffany recounted a class assignment that would impact the rest of her career. The recruit was required to throw a heavy twenty-four-foot ladder from the ground to a standing position on the wall. This practice is commonly known as a ladder throw. It is difficult, and Tiffany admits that she was struggling. There is no specific policy on how to "throw the ladder." According to Tiffany, it had been common practice to throw it a certain way "because that's how males do it."

A female instructor saw her and a few classmates struggling, walked over to them, and said, "You know, you don't have to do it the way they do it. You have to do it the way you can." For Tiffany, the lightbulb went on, or as she describes it, she had "an aha moment." This tip allowed her to explore options she had not considered.

The instructor continued, "You can do the job. You will never be as strong as them. You will not have the upper body strength of a man. But you have smarts and the stature to figure out how to use your body and the things that work for you to get the job done."

Tiffany's lesson in that experience served her continuously throughout her career. Tiffany took her instructor's statement, applied it to her job, and found ways to plot her path. Tiffany's career paralleled the meaning behind Robert Frost's poem "The Road Not Taken." In essence, every journey has multiple paths. Choose the one that works best for you. It will impact your experience and get you to your destination.

After graduating from recruit school, she "just wanted to be good at her job and provide for her daughter." She was the only female at her first fire station. She worked there for a few years and felt part of the team. She was comfortable and had no aspirations for promotion. But her close network of firefighters saw things differently.

Those firefighters were a group of African American men with different personalities. The group dynamics ranged from spiritual to a "fight them at the gates Malcolm X" type. She valued their opinion, and the group served the dual roles of network and mentors. They encouraged her to seek the first promotion. She wasn't interested. She "didn't want to rock the boat."

They sat her down and told her, "It was time," and that she had learned everything she needed about firefighting. She continued to fight their suggestion until it clicked. "Why have mentors if you are unwilling to listen?" The team laid out the path to promotion for her. She knew it wouldn't be easy, but she went for it.

She dedicated four to five months to preparing for the exam. Seventy to eighty persons tested when she did. The results were in, and she was the number one candidate—a first in the history of Prince George's County. She was thrilled about her accomplishments and expected those around her to be happy, too. After all, she was well-liked and never had any problems.

The reaction from other fire safety professionals in Prince George's County was a surprise. How could she be the number one candidate? The fire service conducted an internal investigation because they accused her of cheating. For the first time in her career, she felt like a minority. Before this point, there was no indication that her skin tone or gender would affect her treatment in the department.

Why were they pushing back? She had worked hard and earned this just like anyone else. On the day of the promotion, the testers sat in front of the room in rank order, with her in the number one seat. She could feel the energy of animosity of everything going on behind her. It was instantaneous, and she felt anxiety rising within her. She couldn't allow what she was feeling to stand in her way. She stayed focused and remembered that she had committed herself to doing what was necessary for success in her career. She had earned her spot through hard work and discipline.

After promotion, she spent two years as a lieutenant, where she experienced the success and mistakes that come with your first managerial role. Her team of mentors supported her through those years and encouraged her to prepare for promotion. Again, it was not on her radar as she had just started to feel comfortable in her leadership role, but she listened and applied.

Lightning would strike again. The first time Tiffany was successful, the department minimized her top test score as a fluke, but now they would have to pay attention to her. It would not be positive attention. Once again, she was the number one candidate after tallying the test results. The expectation is that high-scoring candidates can select their assignments. However, while the top male candidates had that option, she did not. They told her where and when to show up. They transferred her and moved her around. She would not refuse. They could not break her. She accepted the assignments and approached her work with excellence and professionalism.

She relied on her spiritual foundation and relationship with God to cope with the stresses of moving around and to handle the racism she experienced. She believed God was opening doors and preparing her, so mentally, she decided "to just be open to change." She remained grace under fire.

Tiffany continued as the top candidate in subsequent promotional exams. She served in many capacities throughout her career, and each one prepared her for the ultimate position. One of the most rewarding experiences for her was serving as the battalion chief in the fire safety training department that included recruit school. The work in that organization touched her deeply. When she began the new position, her mind transported her back to recruit school, where she remembered her feelings and the insightful instructor who provided one tip that "gave us the path on how to get through recruit school."

She spent four years in training. She had first-hand experience of what it meant to be a woman in the fire service. She knew the recruit school marked "the first experience a woman has in the fire service. Female recruits need to see women in leadership—women who encourage them and tell them that they can do the job. Let me show you how to do it. Don't do it like they're doing it. Find your way."

Because of this, she taught male instructors that there are different ways to accomplish tasks in school. She also worked with the cadet program and introduced high school students in the community to the fire service. Her work in the program inspired ten young women to join the fire service. Recruits have said, "We wouldn't be here if it weren't for you." Tiffany's humility will not accept that. She believes "she just opened the door."

However, they continued to second-guess and question her.

Her journey led her to the position of the first African American Female Fire Chief of Prince George's County. Though she earned her title, she is still not considered equal to male fire chiefs.

Tiffany states, "They have the loyalty. They have all the things that come with their color and gender in the fire service. A white male chief in the fire services is regarded way higher than me, even though I work ten times harder, and I have to be more accurate."

At times, she described her career as "a constant fight." She refused to back down from the fight. She had done nothing wrong and proved it to them through her work, even though the situation scared her. "There was always fear. It was part of the job."

People's lives depended on her doing her job well. She learned to harness the fear and use it to propel her. She used her expertise, confidence in her abilities, and skillset to keep pushing forward in the face of adversity, just like you do when you fight a fire.

## Perseverance Defined

Perseverance is persisting in a task or goal despite difficulties, setbacks, or obstacles. It requires a willingness to stay focused and keep going despite challenges and obstacles (Shaffner 2020). Progress may be slow, but you keep moving forward.

People who demonstrate perseverance tend to be highly motivated, goal-oriented individuals who can maintain focus and commitment in adversity. They are often willing to take on challenging tasks and see setbacks and failures as opportunities for growth and learning rather than as reasons to give up.

A recent article by Bergland highlighted that dopamine is a neurotransmitter that plays a crucial role in motivation and perseverance. It generates feelings of satisfaction and reward when we achieve goals necessary for survival and reproduction, and dopamine receptors act as gateways for forming excellent and bad habits. Individuals with higher dopamine levels tend to persist in achieving nonbiological goals through hard work and perseverance, which releases dopamine (2011).

Those with low dopamine levels can feel unmotivated and apathetic. Still, ways to increase dopamine production include dividing big goals into smaller ones, visualizing success, imposing deadlines, and celebrating small wins, reinforcing motivation and drive to persevere (Bergland 2011).

Tiffany refused to let others' opinions of her race and gender stand in her way. Her perseverance and resilience kept her focused on her goals, and ultimately, she received the highest ranking in the fire service. Similarly, demonstrating perseverance helped me overcome fear and take on the next career opportunity.

"You successfully led a team to complete an important project, a role normally reserved for a senior engineer."

I felt a smile forming on my lips as I read the words from the award I received. This began my history of volunteering for work assignments in the face of fear. The success and growth I experienced reinforced my belief that I could figure things out. I would remember this experience and the feeling of success as I pondered opportunities throughout my career.

It was cliche, but you could cut the tension with a knife.

We had all been standing around the equipment room, an ample open space with electronic equipment racks lining the room. The room was cool to keep the equipment from overheating. Scattered throughout the room, you could see boxes, unopened crates, and the tools necessary to continue installing new systems.

Approximately ten engineers and electronics technicians stood around for the morning huddle, awaiting the arrival of the manager to start the meeting. We dressed in electronics chic, including jeans, boots, sneakers, and the occasional baseball hat. You couldn't tell the senior engineers from someone in my position as a technician. The equipment's hum mixed with the conversation chatter to create a quiet background noise.

The manager of the technical support unit arrived and began the meeting with an update on construction and a discussion about the project's next steps and timelines. It was essential to commission the building and to open on time. The project planning had taken several years, and missing the opening date would cause cost overruns and possible operational impacts. The stakes were high with local and federal political interest.

He highlighted that one significant effort remained: installing and validating communications lines. Approximately seventy-five circuits needed testing. Without working inter and intra phone lines, employees could not complete all aspects of their position. Looking around the group, he said he needed someone to lead the testing and provide a daily status.

The room went quiet, and you could feel a rush of nervous energy as we eyed each other sideways. Would he select someone, and who would it be? Greg stood there, letting the silence grow louder, and I could feel the moisture forming in the palms of my hands. No one moved or said anything until I broke the silence. "I will do it."

Those four words relieved the tension in the room.

The experience of leading the team allowed me to practice collaboration, listen to and resolve problems, and brief senior managers.

I collaborated with the team to develop a schedule for testing each line and worked with each external location to ensure the completion of work with minimal impact. We encountered minor hiccups during our testing. Given the passage of time, I cannot recall specifics. However, I remember we delivered on time.

This experience pushed me outside of my comfort zone. I had always been a team member, but this was my first experience as a team lead. A young Black female technician leading a team of engineers was not a common sight. I only understood the significance of my volunteering once I received an award for the project's leadership. The write-up with the award stated that I stepped up to lead, "a role that was generally reserved for a senior engineer."

## Importance of Perseverance

Perseverance is a valuable quality in life, both professionally and personally. It can help you overcome obstacles, accomplish goals, and experience more success. It is vital to balance perseverance with resiliency and know when to seek guidance.

A 3,294-participant study conducted over eighteen years on adults with an average age of forty-five found that individuals who don't quit on themselves have lesser anxiety (Bergland 2019). The key finding is that goal perseverance and optimism improve mental health outcomes over time. Maintaining determination and positivity creates resilience against anxiety, depression, and panic disorders by providing a sense of purpose and meaning (American Psychological Association 2019).

For women of color, perseverance is a crucial trait. In the face of obstacles, we must continue moving toward our goals while overcoming and destroying the systemic barriers and unique challenges we face. Without fortitude, we may find ourselves in unfulfilling or unrewarding careers. We must courageously use our voices to advocate for ourselves, our communities, and others in the face of adversity. We must destroy the barriers to create pathways for the generations coming behind us.

# PART III

# TAKING IT TO
# THE NEXT LEVEL

———

CHAPTER 9

# BUILD YOUR BRAND: BECOME THE OBVIOUS CHOICE

———

"I think what really turned the table for me is that I had set some standards."

Before she became known for her approach to leading, Teresa began building her persona based on consistent professionalism and positivity in the face of obstacles. It wasn't always easy. It had been two months, and the situation was unbearable.

The sexual harassment had gotten so bad that she needed to seek help. She was a cop and accustomed to inappropriate jokes and comments. However, this was too much. He was her supervisor. "I started getting to the point where when I saw him, I would get these chills. I started calling in sick."

He was phoning her at work and would show up on the street when she worked. One day, he pulled alongside the car she and her partner were in and told her how he would ravish her body. Her partner was appalled and commented that this was sexual harassment.

His response was unbelievable. "The supervisor told my partner, 'You mind your own business. I've got long pockets. I don't care about sexual harassment. My dad told me if I see something I like to go after it.' No. I said, 'Well, your dad didn't know me.'"

She was young, relatively inexperienced, and didn't know how to handle what was happening to her, so she contacted a senior African American male officer who was an attorney and asked for advice. He suggested that she write down all the incidents happening to her and then contact the Equal Employment Opportunity Commission (EEOC) or someone specializing in sexual harassment cases. As luck would have it, the unit she belonged to was dismantled, and she was transferred, never seeing the supervisor who was sexually harassing her again.

Reaching out to that senior officer put her on his radar. Due to her positive attitude and how she discussed the harassment with him, he became her mentor and helped her rise in the ranks to the highest position in the agency. She attributed much of her success to what she learned from him and her cheerful demeanor.

Her mentor told her two essential things. "Get your degrees and do the right thing for the right reason. Then you don't have to worry." Education was a prerequisite for any leadership position in the department, so she followed his advice and got her bachelor's and master's degrees while working full time and raising young children.

She had not considered moving into a management position until he became her mentor, but with his input, she learned to see things differently. When they would meet different people, and she would call someone a butthole, his response was, "That's why you need to get promoted, so you don't have to work for somebody like that." That's how her path to management positions started. He helped her understand that fewer people were above her for every promotion she received. That idea kept her moving forward, and she wouldn't allow negativity in the environment to distract her.

His advice reinforced what she had learned from her father. She learned valuable life lessons from her parents and sister. Positive experiences influenced her values, like her dad instilling the importance of acting with integrity. Yet the tragic loss of her parents' twins also shaped her beliefs. They welcomed another child they cherished deeply. She became their world. However, it seemed they had little time for her Teresa.

"My aunt used to always tell me that they would leave me in a bedroom crying and would take my sister with them. I was always left behind. I guess I kind of learned how to treat people the way I wanted to be treated." As if that wasn't bad enough, Teresa and her sister did not have a good relationship growing up. It seemed to Teresa that her sister had jealousy in her heart, and Teresa didn't know why. Teresa made a decision. "I just wanted to be different. Because when you are jealous like that, to me, you have to be living a life of anger. You're mad at something or somebody."

Her consistently positive attitude and professional treatment of people stood out from her colleagues and became her hallmark. It helped her build positive relations between the union and management when general distrust lay between the two groups. Her employees and coworkers knew what to expect from her.

"I try to listen whenever they come to me with issues. I want to listen first and then offer some advice that'll help. At least you know I care because I'm listening." Her approach to human relations was the foundation of her leadership style. It was also why her mentor asked her to follow him when he left to head another agency.

He used his authority to create a position for her, and with that act, her mentor moved into the sponsor role. She accepted the offer and retired from her agency. They had developed a relationship of trust. He knew her brand, and she was the type of leader he wanted on his team.

The new agency was not as challenging as where she left, but it was different. She didn't have first-hand knowledge of the culture because she had not worked through the ranks in the new agency. She also had to build a network. That was challenging because she was an outsider, and there were only a few women. True to her brand, she entered the new organization, built relationships, and accomplished her work with integrity and positivity. Her leadership earned her a promotion to become the first female and first African American female deputy chief.

During her thirty-seven-year law enforcement career, she reached senior leadership ranking in two different law enforcement agencies. She never allowed the sexual harassment or the challenging and paramilitary environment to change who she was or enable the men to silence her. Her leadership style became her brand and helped her excel against the odds.

## Personal Brand Defined

The concept of personal branding is over twenty-five years old. Initially coined by Tom Peters in his *Fast Company* article from 1997, entitled "The Brand Called You." In that article, Tom states, "We each are CEOs of our own companies: Me Inc. To be in business today, our most important job is to be head marketer for the brand called you." What Tom means by this is that you need to know what makes you unique and helps you stand out. "What are the qualities or characteristics that make you distinctive from your colleagues?"

Most people think of branding as being for big companies or organizations. However, branding isn't just for companies. It's about standing out and differentiating yourself (or their product/service) from everyone else. For personal branding, ask: Are you known to show up early and work late? Do you deliver on time and under budget? Are you an effective communicator? Are you a center of influence with your coworkers? Your brand is about you as an individual—what you offer that helps your organization accomplish its mission.

According to Zidar and Maric, "personal branding is the process that takes personality, skills and unique packages and characteristics. When you think on one person, the personal brand is the powerful and clear idea that comes to mind" (2015). We don't tend to think of colleagues in branding terms. Yet when we work with colleagues, we immediately know who they are. We say things like, "that person delivers well, but they leave dead bodies." We also characterize people as buttholes. We also know when we call people effective communicators because they consistently deliver great presentations.

These are all forms of personal branding in terms of your career, and you should spend some time intentionally cultivating the brand you want to build, the brand you want others to associate with you, especially since your brand could work on your behalf when you're not even in the office like it did for Lena.

She had been recovering at home from her surgery for the last few months. It was only two weeks after her return, and the posting for the promotion she wanted was available. What was she going to do? Law enforcement, like other careers, relies on your network. She didn't know the new sheriff, and he certainly did not know her. He had assumed his new office while she was convalescing. She applied for the position, vowing to do her best despite the odds stacked against her.

When Lena set her mind to something, she was unstoppable. Her hard-working family instilled in her a sense of preparedness and taught her the need to go above and beyond to succeed. She applied this knowledge early in life, beginning university at sixteen. She graduated with honors and then pursued her MBA.

"My family is a huge part of me and a huge part of my life, and they've prepared me for what I would face. Life's not fair, and it never will be. People are going to look at you a certain kind of way. You are Black. You're gonna have to do everything 150 percent. You add on the woman and going into a male-dominated profession. Now you have to give 200 percent and do everything double to what these people over here get to sit in their office and do."

Her family ensured she would be independent and thick-skinned with a strong sense of self. This would be of critical importance as Lena would face what was at the intersection of Black, woman, lesbian, and law enforcement officer.

She applied this same get-it-done mentality from her childhood to her career, and after only six years in law enforcement, she was promoted to sergeant, the first management position in the sheriff's office. Her career took off quickly. According to a recent National Institute of Justice special report dated July 2019, entitled "Women in Policing: Breaking Barriers and Blazing a Path," about eighteen thousand law enforcement agencies exist in the United States, and women make up approximately 13 percent of the officers. Of that number, less than 3 percent of chiefs are women.

As a sergeant, she did the job the only way she knew. "Doing the right thing is always of the utmost importance to me, regardless of the people involved in the situation. Those are my boundary lines. Am I doing this honestly? Am I doing it with integrity? Then, of course, you've got to have some professionalism, some respect, and a little compassion." This became her reputation and distinguished her throughout her twenty-five-year public safety (law enforcement) career.

During her career, "I wrote so much discipline in my life, not because I wanted to but because, again, you lead with integrity, I gotta write you up, or I gotta discipline you because this is what I need to do. But I always do it the right way. People don't come and complain about me." She described a situation when an employee refused to follow an order. She counseled him about the expectations and the importance of following rules.

In their world, a refusal to follow rules means people may die. The second time it happened, she compassionately reminded him. He still had not learned the lesson, and it happened a final time. She did not hesitate to reprimand him. He received a punishment of a few days off without pay. In her experience, when you have treated people with compassionate professionalism, they find it easier to accept their punishment.

The first time she met the new sheriff was during her interview. She didn't think her interview was stellar, yet she was selected for the job. She attributed that selection to her reputation for how she accomplished her tasks. Lena found out later that her coworkers and bosses had put her on the sheriff's radar.

"While I was gone, people were talking to the sheriff about me, so they were already kind of helping me along the way." She believed the differentiator in helping her move ahead was: "I had set some standards. I had put the unit that I had taken over that was in a bit of additional disarray in order after about eighteen months." Her bosses and peers saw what she had done, and they talked about it.

She became the second African American woman promoted to deputy chief in the history of the local sheriff's department.

## Importance of a Personal Brand

Building a personal brand is essential because, like Lena, you want people to think immediately of you for specific projects because people know you have the skills and expertise to deliver. For example, suppose the organization wants to implement a new IT solution. In that case, you want your name recommended because you are known for delivering projects on time and under budget.

"When your true talents are understood, it's far more likely you'll be tapped for relevant and interesting assignments, and it helps you stand out in a field of competitors. Research by Sylvia and Hewlett at the Center for Talent Innovation shows that cultivating your personal brand is one of the best ways to attract a sponsor, and professionals with sponsors are 23 percent more likely than their peers to get promoted" (Clark 2018).

While true for all women, it is critical for women of color. Women of color often have all the boxes checked and are prepared professionals, yet they have difficulty moving forward. Personal branding will help them do that.

As you've no doubt seen throughout the stories shared in this book, sponsors and mentors are a crucial way to be seen and get promotions. They are willing to bring your name into conversations that you ordinarily wouldn't be brought into. Those individuals know and rely on your brand.

One of the reasons that developing an intentional brand is uniquely challenging for women is that "gender norms presume that women should be agreeable, warm and nurturing and when they violate these norms—such as when they step up to make a tough decision, share a strong opinion or promote themselves—they're often penalized for that behavior in a way that men wouldn't be" (Clark 2018).

In other words, women, particularly women of color, who are assertive and aren't afraid to speak their minds are seen negatively and called derogatory names. Despite gender norms, sponsors and mentors can vouch for bold women's qualifications and qualities to overcome stereotypes.

If you want to be known, it's time to get intentional about creating a career brand that represents who you are and can open doors for you. Some specific ways to develop a brand include:

1. You need to understand who you are and share your authentic self. What skills do you have? What are your values, and what are you passionate about? What skills do you need to develop?

2. How do people experience you? This is important because you may think people see and know you for one thing, only to find out they don't. Seek feedback from sources like colleagues, friends, and family who know you. Ask them questions such as: How would you describe me to someone new? What are my strengths? What are my weaknesses? If people are not experiencing you how you want to be known, you need to make a change.

3. You need to understand the environment where you are. What is your organization's culture? What is your organization expected to deliver? What behaviors and skills does your organization value?

4. Determine what you want to accomplish in your career. Do you want the top position, and if so, how do you get there? You can learn by reading the organization's blogs or website or talking to others with more tenure in your organization. Ask for an informal meeting with senior leaders to understand their roles and how they got into their positions. This will help you learn about the organization's various roles and provide insight into your desired jobs. As you meet with leaders, pay attention to how they communicate, their influence, how they exercise power, and what they believe is important and critical in the organization. This will teach you what is needed to get there. From there, you can build a roadmap for

your career. Preparation may mean volunteering to take on additional projects or seeking further training in the office. It may mean additional education outside the office or volunteering to develop skills you currently don't have.

You need to understand that you are a brand and begin thinking about all the decisions you make about your career. For women of color, this is critical to move you from entering your career onto the first rung of management.

Wensil and Ernst interviewed thirty-seven executive women to understand how they maintained momentum in spite of obstacles. Eighty-three percent said, "Clarity of purpose and brand management was crucial" (2023). It's also about how you get your work done and the quality of the work you deliver. You should consistently deliver value regardless of the opportunity. Doing so is crucial to establishing your brand, advancing your career, and navigating different job opportunities.

The officers highlighted in this chapter were known for consistently showing up. Peers, employees, and superiors knew how these women delivered, which ultimately opened doors for them. Learn from their examples so you can be recognized within your organization.

## CHAPTER 10

# IT'S WHO YOU KNOW: BUILDING YOUR NETWORK

———

Someone once said she was the "Alexandria Ocasio-Cortez (AOC) of the New York Metropolitan Transit Authority."

The concrete jungle, the Big Apple, or whatever nickname you use for New York City gave birth to her curiosity and, ultimately, her career. The city and summers traveling the US provided the backdrop to frame Veronica Vanterpool's worldview. An avid observer, she took note of the physical differences of the communities she visited and would always ask herself one question. "Why does our community look the way it does when others don't?"

She grew up in New York City surrounded by community parks paved for basketball and handball courts but with little greenery. "And made for some very bad falls off the seesaw." The differences she saw would spark her desire to pursue environmental science and policy. Her understanding of these environmental differences would grow to form her "core value or a core principle, and that has really been equity."

She began her career working in an international nonprofit organization in the environmental sector. As her career blossomed, she wanted to work in advocacy and policy development, something the organization where she was employed didn't do. For her, there has been a "very strong nexus between the environmental sector and the transportation sector. They're inextricably linked. For me, they've never been divorced. They've never been separate." This caused her to seek employment working on policy at a transportation nonprofit, the beginning of her career in the transportation sector.

"The synergy of this new job in transportation with my background in the environmental field was to reduce greenhouse gas emissions. Yet you can't encourage people to drive less without ensuring viable alternatives exist to a car, like public transit, walking, and biking safely within your community as well as finding affordable housing near transit hubs. Again, that nexus, that core value of equity, brought me into this work." In this nonprofit, she started public policy engagement.

As Veronica delved deeper into the transportation system, she couldn't help but notice the inherent biases and inequalities. That's when she decided to focus her efforts on dispelling these myths and misconceptions. Data clearly showed that increasing funding for public transit would greatly benefit marginalized communities, such as low-income individuals, people with disabilities, seniors, students, and people of color, who rely disproportionately on public transportation. Veronica's work and advocacy in transportation would catch the attention of women in leadership roles who would play a pivotal role in her career.

While Veronica was busy advocating for the community, the transportation nonprofit's executive director would begin preparing her for future opportunities. "She was grooming me from the very beginning unbeknownst to me, and she groomed me by putting me in situations that she knew that I could handle, even before I knew I could handle them, while having confidence that I would always do what was needed to prepare." The two were not in an official mentor-mentee relationship, yet her boss invested her time in developing Veronica. In fact, Veronica moved into the executive director role four years later upon her boss's departure.

Her shift into a focus on transportation occurred when several women were in key leadership positions. Many of these women would help to advance Veronica's career. "When I entered the transportation sector seventeen years ago, several women were in leadership positions as leads of regional transit agencies and authorities and in senior government roles such as secretary of transportation and commissioner. In my early years of advocacy at the nonprofit, I engaged with some of the most powerful decision-makers in public sector transportation. These roles were held by an unprecedented number of women."

Veronica realized she was "their silent mentee" without having an official mentor/mentee relationship with any of them, a term she once heard from a panelist. "I've never officially had mentors, but I've had a network of women around me who have watched me, advanced me, developed me, and promoted me."

The network opened doors that would have been closed to her and accelerated her progress. Another senior official in her network advocated for Veronica to serve as a mayoral appointee on the board of the New York MTA, a position she would hold for nearly four years. Veronica and her organization had been working closely with key transportation agencies and legislators in New York, Connecticut, and New Jersey. They were already known to provide strong advocacy with supporting data.

By this time, she was a fierce opponent who would bring the data to any fight. She expressed her beliefs with much energy and managed not to be stereotyped as the loud, angry Latina. "Advocacy can be contentious, but I think one thing I'm always proud of when I reflect on those days is that I always had the facts. If I was wrong, I said it. I was respectful but tough. Even contentious relationships with some of those women in power did not preclude me from developing helpful relationships with them from which I could learn and from which they served as powerful allies or advocates. I still keep in touch with all of them."

That's not to say that she didn't have a few challenges. Some took exception to her emotive communication style, though it was hard for them to ignore the facts she presented. She once met with an elected official to educate him on the benefits of her proposed project. "My intent was to let him know everything in my brain about this project, just because of the importance of it. He said to me, 'You really do not stop sharing information or talking,' and I said to him, 'I'm sure you're around people who talk to you all day, and I'm not sure you've said that to any of them as you just said to me.'"

Earlier in her career, she was leading a small team of advocates in a meeting with another elected official. "We were talking about a specific public policy proposal. I was making my point, and he said to me, 'Relax,' to which I replied, 'Do not confuse my commitment and dedication to this issue with me being emotional. I do not need to relax. What I'm communicating to you is factual information that I think is important for you to know.' I continued with my discussion topics." When the meeting was over, she thanked him for his time. She believes it's essential to call out condescending behavior and remain steady when belittled or dismissed.

Throughout her career, Veronica knew the importance of preparation and nurturing her strengths. She prided herself on having the data to support her position. Even though she was confident in her abilities, she still had moments when she wished for more confidence.

"I wish I had started with a little bit more confidence, and I don't believe I have ever said that before because I've never really given it that much thought, frankly. But as women, we can overthink decisions. We'll vacillate or tell ourselves no before someone else does. I knew what my strengths were early on. But I wasn't necessarily exercising my strengths in growth opportunities. That is where these women in this network helped develop me."

The research supports Veronica's comment. "Compared with men, women don't consider themselves as ready for promotions. They predict they'll do worse on tests, and they generally underestimate their abilities. This disparity stems from factors ranging from upbringing to biology" (Kay and Shipman 2014).

Veronica benefited from the women in her network, and that support has made it essential for her to give back to other women. "Anyone who reaches out to me, I will respond, particularly if they're a woman." Here's an example. "Many months ago, a young woman I had never met reached out to me on LinkedIn as she and I had a work connection. She explained a little bit about her background and why she wanted to connect and was very apologetic about reaching out. I immediately responded to her to set up a fifteen-minute call. From that call, we had several others, resulting in me inviting her to join a networking event for Latinos. She attended and networked with others. It started with her email, and it continued with my response."

## Networking Defined

Networking is the process of making and maintaining professional relationships with individuals who can offer guidance, support, opportunities, or other benefits related to one's career or business goals. It involves actively seeking out and connecting with people in one's industry or field and cultivating and maintaining those relationships over time.

Networking can take many forms—from attending professional events and conferences to connecting with colleagues and mentors on social media platforms like LinkedIn. Networking aims to build a strong and diverse professional network that can provide support, advice, and opportunities for career advancement or business growth. Effective networking involves being proactive, strategic, and genuine in building and maintaining long-lasting relationships and being willing to offer support and value to others in return.

Networking can provide access to new business opportunities, partnerships, and collaborations that would not have been possible otherwise. It can also help to build a personal brand, establish credibility, and increase visibility within a specific industry or field, something Shannetta Griffin knows all about.

Her communication style was a bit aggressive and forceful. What did they expect? She grew up with six brothers and was used to wrestling, playing football, and standing her ground. She had to be forceful to be heard. As a woman, that communication style is not effective in the work environment. She knew that if she didn't change, it would impact her career negatively.

Shannetta Griffin, P.E. is a seasoned professional, a trailblazer, and the first African American female to graduate from her university with a four-year degree in civil engineering. She was the only Black woman in her program. She chuckled when she reflected on her career. It wasn't necessarily about being an engineer. It was just this idea that "she wanted to build things, and she wanted to help people."

Her career began with a tremendous amount of press, accolades, and words from the governor's office recognizing her educational accomplishments. These types of honors opened doors for her. In her first position out of college, she was fortunate to work for a company where the owner and her manager saw promise in women and gave them opportunities to grow and excel. He was her first ally. With his encouragement, she branched into other engineering areas in transportation, leading her to develop airport projects. Shannetta's husband was in sales and moved around often in his career. Their move created opportunities for her to work in different areas of airport development—something that would benefit her later in her career in a way she didn't expect.

Her next position was working for a Black-owned and male-dominated company, which was challenging because it seemed they didn't support her and didn't want to give her the same opportunities as her male counterparts. She recalls that they consistently helped younger Black men starting with the company. Her tone softened while she explained her sadness at the disrespect by Black men in a Black-owned company. However, she was not going to let them stand in her way. She advocated for herself and delivered her work.

One of the most critical pieces of feedback a mentor gave her was that she had yet to learn the art of communication. Her mentor told her she needed to find a better way to articulate her concerns. It was not what she said but how she said it. She needed to gather facts and present them without emotion. As Shannetta reflected on the advice, she realized while she would speak up in situations, it wasn't always well-received. Maybe that was because she had developed a defensive communication style from those early days with her brothers and in college. Her communication style in the workplace was too much and not well-received.

Shannetta decided that her mentor was correct. She changed her communication style. She prepared for her meetings and would jot down notes to stay focused on the facts. She learned to control her emotions. When she presented challenges, she also offered solutions. This style of engagement caused people in the room to listen and not immediately ignore her. "I learned how to communicate as they communicated, which was to show my level of expertise or show compassion for somebody else in the room. It took some battle scars because I had some tough roads to try and get people to respect me."

After that experience, when one of her mentors gave advice, she listened. This time, the topic was about not going alone. They told her, "Shannetta, we don't do anything in our profession alone. There are tons of ways to get information and meet people. It's all about the people game. It's about who you know and, in a lot of instances, how you make decisions."

As her career progressed, she became intentional with building connections by joining professional associations such as the National Society of Civil Engineers, the National Society of Black Engineers, and several other professional, civic, and social organizations. The relationships she built opened doors for her and helped her secure several positions that people recommended. They also became her clients when she ran her own consulting company.

"Organizations have really been where I've made a lot of these connections. People in these organizations and in companies I worked in became sponsors for me. Those folks would say, 'How about Shannetta.' For example, if they were speaking with someone looking to fill a position, they may say, 'You should reach out to Shannetta Griffin, and here's why.'"

This type of networking has helped her have a fulfilling career, opened doors for her, and placed her in positions that, ordinarily, she wouldn't have been in. The most significant thing that has happened to her is the opportunity for appointment to a critical federal position by the Biden/Harris administration, which would not have happened without her network.

Her friend contacted her and suggested that she apply to be part of the president's administration. That was the furthest thing from her mind, but the person pushed her to go ahead and try it, so she submitted her résumé. At every step of the hiring process, she had people within her network who supported her and said, "You should do this."

Shannetta only realized it in the final interview, but she had broad career experience from her various positions and understood much of the administration's focus. During the interview, she just talked about her expertise and what she had accomplished. With the mentors, allies, and sponsors she developed through her network, she was prepared for the job. She is the first woman of color to lead that organization in the history of that federal agency.

Shannetta's story is similar to yet different from Veronica's. They both have used their expertise to ascend to the most senior levels in the federal government as executives. They both had solid mentors who gave them advice and counsel. They had vital sponsors who opened doors for them, moved them into positions, or spoke their names in meetings behind closed doors. Shannetta's network focused on actual organizations, and Veronica built her network through individual engagements.

Their stories offer a couple of different approaches to building your network. You create one-on-one networks based on engagements with individuals, or you can cultivate networks with individuals based on organizations you both belong to.

Both stories highlight the impact and opportunities networks present to your career. Either way, the power of the network to help you in your career is critical. As I stated in the chapter on overcoming obstacles (setbacks), having a network can help support you during difficult times.

## Reasons People Don't Network

The benefits of networking can be as simple as finding a friend in your field and creating a support network to find career opportunities or clients. However, some people may need help networking or need help seeing the impact not doing it can have.

A weak career network can significantly impact an individual's career growth and opportunities. Research by LinkedIn in 2020 found that "women in the US are 28 percent less likely than men to have a strong network" (Lewis). Some impacts of a weak career network are:

- You may have limited job opportunities because you do not hear about openings, especially if you are looking for a new position. According to Roberts and Mayo, Black professionals often feel that they have to focus on work and work harder than everyone else, so they don't have time to network. The impact is that they are missing out on promotions because the decision-makers don't know them (2020).
- You may miss professional development because word of mouth may not inform you of training opportunities, which may slow or limit professional development.
- A weak network may reduce your visibility, making developing mentor or sponsorship relationships harder. "Networking can be especially challenging for professionals of color, who may not only experience general discomfort, but also face unique challenges from not being perceived as powerful, credible, or resourceful—this deficit-based assessment often results in less outreach and relationship-building" (Roberts and Mayo 2020).

## Build Your Network

Here are some steps to build a strong career network for women of color:

- Join professional organizations and affinity groups specifically for women of color in your industry or your organization. You can learn about the best practices of your field or organization.

- Participate in online communities related to your profession.
- Find mentors who can guide, advise, and support your career journey. You want a mix of mentors—those who are like you and those who are not. For example, in my life, I have had a range of mentors: Black women, Black men, white women, and white men.
- Take full advantage of organization programs. Apply to leadership development and mentorship programs that match you with senior leaders. Send a letter of introduction via email and ask to interview a senior leader to learn more about them. This may begin the start of a working relationship.
- Connect with allies who can use their privilege and influence to advocate for marginalized groups. Allies can help you expand your network, provide access to new opportunities, and endorse you in the workplace.
- Use social media to connect with others in your career field.
- Focus on professional development through workshops and training. This is another opportunity to meet new people in your field or adjacent fields.
- Networking is a two-way street. Provide value to members of your network by sharing information, expertise, and resources or volunteering to help.
- Follow up and stay in touch with people you meet by calling, texting, or social media. Networking is about building relationships.

Given the unique challenges women of color face, it is essential for them to build a strong network. Networking can help create relationships with other professionals who can provide advice, mentorship, and sponsorship as we overcome workplace barriers. Networks can also provide access to opportunities and increased visibility. A key advantage for women of color is challenging stereotypes by building relationships with others in their field, showcasing their skills, helping others see their value, and overcoming stereotypes.

## CHAPTER 11

# TRIFECTA: THE POWER OF MENTORS, ALLIES, AND SPONSORS

---

You can be one too.

"As the only white family, we got stared at, and everything we did was more amplified. I think it helped me realize what it's like when you're the only." This experience gave Abby a sense of what it's like to be the sole member of your race in an environment and began the foundation of her work as an ally, mentor, and sponsor.

Allies, mentors, and sponsors—the words are not interchangeable. Allies work to dismantle systems of oppression in the workplace for the marginalized. Mentors generally provide guidance, advice, and counsel in a one-on-one relationship. A mentor can become a sponsor, but there is a fine line between them. The sponsor is the differentiator for women of color. The person in this role truly has skin in the game. They are willing to risk their reputation to advance a woman of color. Each function is unique and, collectively, creates new realities for women of color at work.

## Ally Defined

The term "ally" typically refers to individuals who actively support and advocate for the rights of the marginalized in the workplace, and their role is defined as allyship. They recognize the systemic barriers to advancement for women of color and actively work to remove the barriers for all members of the workplace. They look for opportunities to amplify the voices of women of color and use their position and influence to try and change the system. They're changing policies for the good of everyone in the group.

While they may be motivated due to a personal connection with one or more group members, they focus on a more significant systemic change in the organization. Criticism against the term ally and allyship suggests that it doesn't imply action. There's a call to change the term ally to coconspirator. "Coconspirators collaborate with women of color to improve the status of the underdog. They work together to achieve racial and gender equity (Smith and Nkomo 2021, 270).

The article "Moving Beyond Performative Allyship: A Conceptual Framework for Anti-racist Coconspirators" argues that the popular concept of "allyship" does not go far enough to address systemic racism. The authors explain that allyship often involves performative actions like using social justice buzzwords or making social media posts without taking substantive action. They contend that moving beyond this shallow, self-serving allyship is necessary to become an "anti-racist coconspirator." Anti-racist coconspirators actively commit to fighting racism through direct action and personal sacrifice. They focus on dismantling oppressive systems, not just helping oppressed groups (Ekpe and Toutant 2022, 67-91).

## Mentor Defined

The term "mentor" typically refers to an experienced and trusted advisor who provides guidance, support, and career advice. A mentor can be someone within or outside the organization with expertise and experience in a particular field or area. "Mentorship is a relationship between someone sharing knowledge and providing guidance (the mentor) and someone learning from that person's experience and example (the mentee)" (Omadeke 2021). Mentors help women of color navigate the complexities of the workplace, providing advice on career development, skill-building, networking, and professional growth.

Mentors also serve as role models, sharing their experiences and lessons learned, inspiring women of color to pursue their professional goals. They can provide critical feedback and help women of color build their confidence and resilience in facing challenges and setbacks. Recent research supports the impact of mentors.

A 2021 quantitative, cross-sectional study investigated the impact of mentorship on the career advancement of two hundred women in the South African public sector. The researchers tested four hypotheses related to dimensions of mentorship—female mentors, career support, mentoring policies, and leadership development. Statistical analysis found a strong positive relationship between career support and advancement as well as between mentoring policies, leadership development, and career advancement.

However, there was no significant relationship between having a female mentor and advancement. The study highlighted the need for formal mentoring programs. Only 4.5 percent of respondents indicated their organization had one. Yet the women viewed mentorship as necessary, with 85.5 percent acknowledging it can increase career advancement. The results indicate dimensions of mentorship like career support and leadership development positively impact women's career advancement in the South African public sector (Mcilongo and Strydom).

## Sponsor Defined

The term "sponsor," when used in reference to women of color at work, typically refers to a senior-level executive or individual in a position of power or influence within an organization who actively advocates for and supports the career advancement of a woman of color. Sponsors "are senior-level champions who hold power in an organization. They use their social capital and credibility to advocate for their protégés and better position them to advance in the workplace. They expect to see a return on their investment in an individual" (Patel 2017).

An individual who has a sponsor is termed a protégé. "A sponsor may put their protégé's name on the table for a promotion or have the power to advocate for their work when they are not in the room or invited to the "important" meeting themselves" (Omadeke 2021). A sponsor is essential for women of color in the workplace, as they often face unique challenges and barriers to advancement.

According to a recent 2021 Gallup article entitled "Closing the Gender and Race Gaps in North American Financial Services," women of color continue to experience minimal gains from job start to a supervisor position. In fact, for every one hundred men promoted, Black and Hispanic women rates were thirty-five and sixty-five, respectively (Elligrud et al.). Sponsors can help mitigate these challenges and provide much-needed support, clearing a pathway for women of color to attain their goals successfully.

In the research for the book *Our Separate Ways: Black and White Women and the Struggle for Professional Identity*, coauthors Ella Bell Smith and Stella M. Nkomo (2021) found that having a sponsor was critical to the success of women of color. They found "someone in the organization who championed their interests and publicly endorsed and advocated for their movement to higher positions" more important than having a mentor (167-168).

Chow's 2021 article "Don't Just Mentor Women and People of Color. Sponsor Them" provides an expanded definition of sponsorship that includes the audience and the protégé and sponsor. Chow outlines specific actions that sponsors can take to influence the audience's actions in support of the protégé, which she calls the ABCDs of sponsorship.

- Amplifying: Promoting a protégé's achievements and successes to help improve their reputation and public image.
- Boosting: Vouching for a protégé's future potential and readiness

- Connecting: Facilitating relationships between the protégé and influential people
- Defending: Challenging negative impressions of the protégé

These actions help override biases and racism that women of color face toward advancement.

## Voices of the Trifecta

In this book, we have listened to the voices of women of color. Now, we will focus on the perspectives of allies, mentors, and sponsors who work from within the system to support, uplift, and advance the careers of women of color. You will also learn that some women who continue this work do so despite the personal impact it may have on their careers. The sponsor plays the most crucial role in promoting the careers of women of color.

If you are interested in playing a critical role in the life of a woman of color and want to learn how to do so, look to the following individuals for inspiration.

### Abigail Smith Ally, Mentor, Sponsor

Abby's early life as the only white family in an African American environment gave her ringside seats to what it's like when no one else looks like you. They moved south when her father accepted a position as a professor at Oakwood College, a historically Black religious institution now known as Oakwood University. She remembers going to church in the community and the sense of community she felt even as people stared at them. "As the only white family, we got stared at, and everything we did was more amplified. I think it helped me realize what it's like when you're the only." This experience gave her a sense of what it's like to be the sole member of your race in an environment and would begin the foundation of her social justice platform.

She didn't realize that her experience was unique until she visited her family, who also lived in the South, and experienced them using racial slurs. The language was emotionally upsetting and brought Abby to tears. She questioned her mother, wanting to know why people would talk like that. She stood up to her cousins because she thought it was wrong, and this was where her standing up for her beliefs began.

She had a similar experience, but it was frightening. Some Black college students were riding with her family and stopped for a bio break at a gas station. The owner came out and pointed a gun at her mother's face and shouted an explicative at them about the Black people riding with them. They quickly drove away. These moments are etched in her memory and cemented in her who she wanted to be.

She learned important lessons from her mother. Abby watched as her mother confronted and overcame gender bias during the seventies. With a bachelor's degree, Abby's mother qualified to be a secretary, but her mother refused to accept societal norms. As her mother climbed in her career, she became an ally and sponsor of the marginalized, creating a work environment that represented the diversity of the USA. This became Abby's norm. Her mother's efforts inspired Abby to do the same.

She didn't understand the racism and the bigotry. She could see the difference in how people look physically and the different complexion colors. But it wasn't until she was in college that she understood the deepness of the impacts of racism and conscious and unconscious bias. Even when it was not easy, she stood for what was important, no matter if there was a price to pay.

To her, the bottom line is that it takes some courage because it is easy to say nothing. She believes that doing nothing is as harmful as actively participating in injustice. A visit to the Holocaust Museum in Washington, DC, in 1994 profoundly impacted her. When she got to the bottom floor, she found a quote that struck her. It read, "They took the Jews, and I said nothing. And then they came for the gypsies, and I said nothing. They came for the homosexuals, and I said nothing. Then they came for the cripples, and I said nothing. Then they came for me." This quote spoke to her, and she realized remaining silent was complicit.

"When we start to normalize the abnormal, and it becomes normal, we are all in a perilous situation." It hurts all of us, putting our communities in jeopardy. Seeing injustice triggers Abby and compels her to speak up and take action. She is keenly aware that her actions may cause a backlash, and there may be repercussions. She has a bit of fear and questions whether she will have to pay a price. The fears don't deter her. She continues anyway.

Abby acknowledges that many have not experienced the poignant racial moments that have contributed to her worldview. She says applying emotional intelligence is necessary to see and understand what's happening to people. Never shy and never meeting a stranger, when Abby sees someone who appears left out of the meeting or conversation, she will ask them directly if they need help or have a mentor. This is one way she develops mentor/mentee relationships, and it's her way of building community. She helps someone, and in turn, they learn to reach out and help others.

While Abby mentors others, it has not always been easy for her. She has had setbacks and professional disappointments. She has had to summon her resilience muscle to keep going, recognizing what was in her span of influence and trying to make the change there. As Abby calls it, navigating "white man's land" can be challenging. An ally stepped in and affirmed Abby's commitment to staying true to herself. He told her he needed her to be her, that her brand of executive was just what his team needed. This was a spark that encouraged Abby to keep moving forward.

Understanding where people are coming from and their struggles is Abby's gift. She can see and listen to people, building connections and establishing trust. She believes this is the opportunity to make a difference in people's lives. She has sponsored countless individuals by creating opportunities for them and selecting them for key roles. Abby is an executive leader with more than thirty years of experience working in a federal agency. She uses her time, energy, and expertise to encourage, develop and support others.

## Nancy Kalinowski, Ally, Mentor, Sponsor

Nancy's childhood was seen through international eyes and profoundly impacted her development. She had the opportunity to live internationally with parents who taught her to be comfortable with different races, genders, ethnicities, and socioeconomic levels. She saw people in extreme poverty, which taught her about economic privilege. It was just how things were, so she didn't have to learn to see and support others who were different later in her life. That was her life, but others didn't see it that way.

She recounted her experience in college from 1970-1974. One of her first roommates was a Black woman. She and Nancy got along well and had no problems. This was during the days of the Black Power movement, and her roommate took a lot of crap for befriending Nancy. Classmates wanted to know how the roommate could live with a white woman, and they encouraged the roommate to move out.

The Blacks and whites would not mingle, and Nancy thought, *How can we get to know each other if we can't sit and talk? How can we feel comfortable with each other?* Her roommate told her, "We're just not there yet. You may be, and I may be, but most people here are not there. She said maybe ten years from now, we'll be there." Nancy responded, "I think that's short-sighted on their part."

Nancy equates her college experience to working for a federal agency. She thinks she saw fear in some people about reaching out to minorities, whether women or men, because they weren't sure if they could relate to the person. What if I say something wrong? What if I'm misconstrued here? In her view, these questions and that fear made it challenging for white people to connect with others. Nancy believes it is easier if a person is in an official mentoring program. Because it's an official program, she thinks that if paired with someone, it's okay to talk to them.

Nancy's early experiences created an openness and curiosity about people. She would read about Black history, listen to the stories of the Civil Rights Movement, and talk to her parents and friends who actually participated in the movement when she was overseas. This is where she learned about white privilege. "It was something early on that I knew was real." Even at work,

Nancy realized it was easier for a white woman to get through the glass ceiling than for a woman of color.

Nancy has been instrumental in uplifting women and women of color. She has been an ally, a mentor, and a sponsor. She believes that to inhabit those roles effectively, you must get to know someone by starting with light conversations like hobbies or other interests and slowly moving to more profound subjects.

"You have to realize that some cultures are more reserved, especially if you're outside their community." If you don't know the person, you cannot sponsor them. "To feel truly comfortable about not thinking of them as here's a Black woman but instead just think this is Angela, who would be perfect for the job. Oh, yeah, I guess she is Black. You gotta get to where you don't think about it in terms of race. You have to think about the best person because you want to increase diversity. You want to increase opportunity. We want to ensure that people who might not normally be seen and perceived by most of the population [know] they've got someone lighting a candle for them."

Nancy is a retired executive who spent over forty years in the federal government, where she positively impacted the lives of many people, including women of color.

## Jodi McCarthy, Ally, Mentor, Sponsor

"A leadership team can't, or government can't represent all the people if only a certain slice of people are leading the effort."

Jodi spent thirty-six years serving the American people in the USAF and a federal agency. Her early career experience when one of her managers set out to prove that as a woman, she was not capable of learning and performing her job because of the "left brain, right brain theory" laid the foundation for the championing of women and minorities in her career. Instead of genuinely learning her position and learning her way around her new town, she worked under extreme pressure, fighting to prove that she could do her new job.

Her story differs from Abby's and Nancy's, yet she has mentored, allied, and sponsored women of color and people of color. As a child, she did not have experiences that exposed her to people of different ethnicities. "My family was not particularly open to embracing other cultures." Jodi recalls that her graduating high school class of about four hundred had only a handful of minorities.

When she entered the United States Air Force, Jodi found that for the first time in her life, she was in the minority. "It was a very new experience for me. Despite how I had been brought up or my limited exposure, I just wasn't intimidated. I met all these different people. Instantly, I put the past behind me and realized I was open to experiencing other people. I think I maybe narrowly escaped having an opinion ingrained in me." This awakening transformed how she related to people and her perspective on the world.

Jodi believes the military and the public sector are "meant to represent every American. It doesn't say just men or just whites. It's for everybody. You can't look at leadership, a team, or a construct that only represents one demographic or two or three. The government has a diverse workforce, and the leadership must reflect that makeup. Because without that, we don't have the whole story. We don't have our entire perspective of the people trying to make government work if the leadership is only a slice of the types of people that are there."

From her days in the USAF and throughout the rest of her life, Jodi intentionally built relations and created a diverse network and group of friends. Called an empath by some, she has the ability to connect and understand others on an emotional level, but she realizes no matter how she relates, she cannot know what it is like to walk in the shoes of a woman of color. "The closest I can come to knowing that is to surround myself with people with various experiences, backgrounds, and cultures. That's the best I can do or any ally can do."

Allying and mentoring may be one of the easier roles of supporting a woman of color. It becomes more challenging when you step into the sponsor role because sponsoring a woman of color often comes with personal and professional risks. Jodi recounted a time when she wanted to select a non-white person for a senior leadership position, and she received a lot of pushback from colleagues. She had to stand her ground because she believed it was the proper selection. She reflected on the different impacts she experienced if the choice wasn't the best fit. In her experience, if a white male was selected and it didn't work out, the story was that he wasn't ready, and there would be no judgment on all white men.

Conversely, if a minority is unsuccessful, there's judgment about gender, race, or ethnicity. Knowing that a lousy selection reflects poorly across a whole group adds additional pressure. "Supporting women is noble, but it does not come with a bunch of pats on the back. It does come with some pushback. It does come with some people close to me in my personal life who have often said, 'Oh, you only promote women, or you're part of the skirt mafia.'"

The naysayers' words.

Pushback and pressure never stopped her from doing what was right. Throughout her career, she positively impacted many persons of color, women of color, and women. The experience in her early career changed her. "Had I not had the experiences I had, I may not champion women like I do."

## Jeff Planty Mentor, Sponsor

Jeff sponsors, mentors, and supports women of color, and his upbringing is one of the reasons behind it. His exposure to diverse cultures stemmed from his childhood growing up in a small town in New York. His mother's remarriage to a military man widened their horizons as they traveled around the country and internationally. Jeff's natural curiosity and ability to connect easily with anyone, regardless of gender or race, is why he supports others. He can walk into any room and initiate conversations with people to establish connections.

While he can connect with others, some men are uncomfortable with connecting with women because of fear of sexual harassment accusations. Jeff is cautious when working closely with women. He actively steers clear of any behavior that might appear unprofessional. He knows of sexual harassment, so he doesn't coach or mentor women after work over drinks or dinner. He does not use the potential of sexual harassment as a reason not to support women of color, nor does he allow the fear of personal or professional impacts to stop him.

He doesn't believe he has experienced any impact on the support that he provides. He said he may get labeled a bit, and he had recently read an article "that men who are allied with women can get marginalized themselves or get labeled as a wimp or metrosexual or you run the risk of falling out of the out of the clique with some of your male counterparts."

Working for several senior female leaders, Jeff "started learning that if I'm more self-aware and listen more than talk,

I start hearing things that the women specifically are sharing in the group conversations. What I started noticing was nobody was listening. I'm just very interested in what people have to say, and I think women, in general, bring a completely different perspective to the conversation, and I'm interested."

Jeff has been amplifying the voices of women of color. For example, if he notices a woman sitting quietly, he invites her into the conversation or may support an idea she has vocalized. "I would say socially privileged as a white male. My voice carries a little bit louder, notch on the volume." He uses that voice as an ally for minority women.

As an executive leading a large organization, Jeff uses his position to converse about diversity and equity with his leaders. It's probably not always perfect, but he tries to make it a conversational engagement. For example, he spoke with his team about the angry Black woman trope. He explained why it's unacceptable to quickly label one of the Black female leaders that way and explained to them what that stereotype means. He is working to create an environment where the leaders have a safe space to discuss, learn, and grow.

Because Jeff has never met a stranger, it is relatively easy for him to build a network. His diverse network has allowed him to work on civil rights programs, hiring initiatives, and development programs. He's like a visa, everywhere you want to be. He's regularly sought out to speak on panels, speed mentoring, and any event about people. His network continues growing, but he realizes that women of color also need a network. "It's not always about me making a network connection but connecting other women of color to strengthen their voice."

Jeffrey Planty is an executive leader at a federal agency with nearly forty years of federal service. At the agency where he works, two organizations have acknowledged him. Human resources recognized him as a "champion" of Civil Rights for developing a national program for persons with targeted disabilities. Last year, he received the prestigious Presidential Rank Award, given by the president of the United States.

### Jeffrey Vincent Mentor, Sponsor

"As an African American man, as I was growing up, my father taught me about racial injustice, and he would tell me there would be times that I would encounter situations that would require me to have to be twice as good to be considered equal. That's not fair. Don't pretend that it's fair. Don't get mad that it's not fair. That's just the way it is. Accept it. there's no need to cry about it." He viewed the world through this perspective.

Jeffrey has had a thirty-six-year public sector career between the military and working in a federal agency since the early 1980s. He's risen to an executive position, one of the most senior in government. He has had many successes, and there have certainly been bumps along the way. He describes not getting a fair shake at times.

As difficult as things may have been for him at times in his work environment, Black women often faced similar or worse circumstances. Throughout his career, he can recount times when women, and in some cases specifically Black women, were held to a different standard. Early in his career, he felt powerless to do anything to help.

He believes it can be challenging for Black men to support Black women because they often feel like they could lose their position. To help someone else could mean putting their career in jeopardy. At times, he remained silent when he felt things were unfair. The fear of speaking out results in the same fate as the person in question. "There were certainly times I felt the shame of not saying anything."

Jeffrey has mentored and sponsored countless people throughout his career. As he was promoted in his career, he didn't shy away from selecting who he believed to be the best individual for the job. It didn't matter their gender, race, or ethnicity. When a senior female leader was retiring, she sat down with Jeffrey to chat.

She said to him, "I've watched you. Sometimes, I did not always like what you did, but you've done something that's been very impressive. I've watched you build the management team. And I've been impressed by how you reach out to women and you include women in your management team. It's a well-balanced team. That's not by mistake. Something in you makes you do that." As he reflected, there certainly was.

It goes back to his early career. Jeffrey thinks about the impact of his actions on others, especially women, and giving them opportunities. He thinks about the number of people who have helped and supported him. Despite the setbacks, he has had many successes. Those successes would not have occurred without the help and support of others and giving him opportunities. He can help others and ensure a level playing field. Ultimately, all anyone wants, regardless of gender or race, is the opportunity to compete on a level playing field.

The possibility of a sexual harassment charge by someone you are helping is a poor excuse not to help someone. In Jeffrey's opinion, if there is no ulterior motive, it will be apparent to the person you are trying to help. "People can read you, and they will know if you are not truly interested in helping them." He called a flag on this play.

Jeffrey's broad career has given him some unique insights. He believes women of color should "diversify yourselves, master your career field, your job, whatever it is you do and whatever the task is, if an opportunity presents itself, certainly diversify yourself. Don't pigeonhole yourself. Don't get stuck in one location, and don't let anybody label you." His family is important to him. "I would always tell everybody, and I say this to men and women, do not sacrifice your family for a career. Your family always has to come first.

"Sometimes you got to be your spokesperson. However, if you have the opportunity to find a sponsor, you need to have someone who's willing to speak up for you in the room when you're not there." You find a sponsor by excelling in your career field. Jeffrey sponsors others, and others have sponsored him.

The voices shared in this chapter provide inspiration and insight into how allies, mentors, and sponsors can support and advance the careers of women of color. Abby, Nancy, Jodi, Jeff, and Jeffrey demonstrated through their stories that this work requires courage, sacrifice, and a commitment to doing what is right, even when it is difficult. Their experiences highlight the need for more people, especially those in positions of influence, to step up as coconspirators and anti-racist accomplices. The time for performative allyship is over. We must move toward substantive action and change.

The call is clear. We all have a role in dismantling systemic barriers, amplifying marginalized voices, and creating workplaces where everyone, regardless of gender or race, has equitable opportunities to grow, contribute, and lead. The future we build depends on the actions we take today. It's your turn to act and lend your time, voice, and clout to support a woman of color today!

# CONCLUSION

———

We began this journey with a whisper, a hushed stereotype that echoed loudly: "They only hired you to comply with affirmative action." Women of color in the public sector face prejudices and systemic barriers in the public sector. My experience ignited the spark for this book, prompting a deep dive into the daily challenges navigated by those who experience them firsthand. Now, let's examine where we are and revisit the world through the lens of the stories, experiences, and insights we've gathered, laying the foundation for the future.

As of 2022, the number of people employed by local and state governments is approximately 19.2 million. Of that, about 778 thousand are women of color in senior leadership positions (EEOC 2021). It is a paltry number by comparison. The federal government is not much better. Of the 2.1 million federal employees, 22.8 percent of persons of color reach the senior executive service (Office of Personnel Management 2022).

A breakdown of the percentage of women in that number is unknown. The highest-ranking positions in the public sector lack diverse perspectives and experiences, leading to policy creation based on a limited set of experiences. To bring about positive change for marginalized communities, promoting more women of color to critical positions that can develop policies that benefit everyone is crucial.

The challenge is that women of color face systemic barriers, stereotyping, gender bias, and other discriminatory practices that either keep women out of the public sector or trap them in entry-level positions with little impact or influence. The playing field is not level for women of color. If it were, more women of color would be in critical senior leadership positions.

We anticipate the public sector will employ more people of color as their population increases. However, our unfortunate history has shown that this growth does not always lead to a proportional rise in the career advancement of women of color. In other words, even though we expect to see more people of color employed in the public sector, this does not guarantee that women of color will have the same opportunities to advance in their careers.

Throughout this book, we explored the unique obstacles women of color encounter in public service, from discrimination and stereotyping to lack of mentorship and hostile work environments. However, the women featured demonstrated overcoming these systemic barriers through authentic leadership, solid networks and sponsors, strategic career planning, and perseverance. Their stories prove that while the path may be difficult, women of color can ascend to the highest ranks of public leadership.

For women of color to advance, several key themes emerged across the women's experiences that offer a blueprint for success:

- Authenticity is necessary for well-being. Know yourself and lead authentically. The women embraced their true identities and leadership styles despite pressures to conform, building resilience and well-being.
- Use your voice powerfully. Speaking up dismantles stereotypes. Effective use of this skill means you can contribute your lived experiences to deepen the discussion. Be seen, heard, and included.
- Strategically chart your career path: Planning, preparation, and skill development open doors. Opportunities will come. Will you be ready?
- Develop grit and perseverance. Setbacks and failures are inevitable. Reframe them as growth and use that knowledge to keep moving forward.
- Mentors, Allies, and Sponsors—the trifecta provides advice, opportunities, and advocacy. Diverse connections are invaluable.

With the right strategies and support systems, women of color can achieve their highest leadership aspirations in the public sector. Progress means perseverance plus influential sponsorship. While systemic barriers remain, individual women can control their responses, build their skills, and create empowering networks. Their success will also pave the way for more diversity, equity, and inclusion. The women's stories confirmed this theory's core premise. Advancement is possible despite obstacles.

So, what's next? For you, especially if you are a woman of color in the public sector or want to join the public sector, this book is more than a collection of stories and insights. It's a call to action. Challenge the status quo. Seek mentors and be a mentor. Use this book as a tool to break down barriers.

Allies and would-be allies, your role is crucial. Listen, learn, and leverage your positions to enact change. Mentor and sponsor someone who does not look like you. Use your privilege to challenge systemic barriers. Amplify drowned-out voices.

As you close this book, remember the journey is far from over. Let this book be your guide to building bridges, fostering understanding, and creating a more inclusive future in a world that often seems more eager to divide than unite because the journey beyond gender and stereotype is one we must all take together.

The whisper that began this narrative should not be the period at the end of the sentence. It should be the comma that invites more to come. Build a public sector that genuinely represents the public it serves. Now is the time for action.

# ACKNOWLEDGMENTS

---

First, I must thank my husband, Rodney; my son, Phillip; my parents, Michele and Sidney; and my sisters, Karmen and Panella. You encouraged and cheered me along. All of you gave me the strength to carry on in the moments when I wanted to quit. Thanks to friends and family for your texts, for sharing my posts, and for your phone calls.

Thank you to everyone I interviewed for the book and for trusting me to tell your story. I appreciate your time and the perspectives you shared. The beauty of your journey will uplift and empower readers of this book. Thanks to the beta readers who provided feedback and helped to make the manuscript better.

Thanks, "Tash," for introducing me to the group writing program and telling me this year would be amazing for both of us. I would not have embarked on this journey now if it weren't for you. Thanks, Eric Koester, for creating Manuscripts Modern Author Accelerator. Thanks to every editor, instructor, marketing specialist, and designer who helped me through the program. Thanks to my fellow authors in the program who encouraged and celebrated me throughout our journey together. Because of you, I never had to write alone. You all are the best.

Thank you to everyone who supported me through the fundraising campaign. Your support is immeasurable:

Lisandra Green
Natasha Durkins
Victoria Wei
Antoinette Francois
Karmen Ramirez
Panella Page
Joy Little
Nikki Watson
Jay Little
Patricia Gilbert
Anita Enriquez
Janet Scott
Jonathan Fisher
Eric Koester
Ruby Lewis
Terria Garner
Alice Haynes
Stephanie Braxton
Jodi McCarthy
Angela Wilson
Gaylynn Fields
Antoinette Penny
Natalie Blanchard

Sharon Rushing
Sharon Crumley
Maurice Hoffman
Keytoria King
Mark Mcclardy
Tamara Smith
Arlene DeSilva
Jacqueline Shackleford
Vera Northcutt
Bridgette Simmonds
Maria Calhoun
Lynn Ray
Amr Mandour
Julie Browne
Alyce Hood-Fleming
Michelle Sabatini
Franklin Black
Stephanie Gadson
Linda Pharr
Michael Beckles
Gary Alexander
Crystal Gavin
Jeffrey Vincent

Shannetta Griffin
Dominique Wallace
TaFwani Corley
Denise Brown
Josue Gonzalez
Marcia Walden
Sidney Crumley
Prakash Subramanian
Hilary Beard
Felicia McIntrye
Chalon Obi
Danielle Lynch
Olivet Smith
Rebecca Guy
Katrina Hall
Craig Magee
Takisha Brown
Cornelius Young
Marc Brown
Thomas Demske
George Crumley
Marseta Dill
Veronica Vanterpool
Ramone Crowe
Kristina Carr
Maureen Woods
Ernestine Witcher
Benita LaMorell
Terry Hennings
Nancy Kalinowski
Kerri Strnad
Jeroskee Outler

Edwaun Durkins
Paula Thaxton
Robert Beck
Matizza Davis
Angela Roberts Calloway
Steven McCullough
Tyrea Simmons
Telecia Lindo-Johnson
Terrence Holmes
Tatiana Machado-Griffin
Richard Simmons
Gwendolyn Farmer
Tiffany Langhorn
Alanna Watkins
Irie Harris
Ken Harris
John Simmons
Jeanetta Lee
Michael Scott
Rick Beal
Michael Johnson
Tonya Coultas
Theresa Peterson
Danese Banks
June Green
Quinten Tolar
Talitha Blake
Lynnette Cain
Letti Cain
Chantee Christian
Nancy Jasa
Jeff Planty

Trini Sherman
Alexandria Davis
Taneesha Marshall
Ronnette Meyers
Rachael Burroughs
Kelly Brown
Seccurra Loyd
Marquita Rugless
Leslie Glascoe
Neysa Isler
Sherlita Hawkins
Linda M Jones
Renee Anderson
Andreese Davis
Talethia Thomas
John St. Pierre
Neirdra Pressley
Domineca Neal
Amber Osmer
Dr. Erica Kristina Reid
Tennille Blackwell
Lady Francois
Maurice Cates

Darnell Jones
William Alexander
Tolonna Gadson
Kimberly Jones
O'Neil Foster
Donna Barnaby
Phillip Tolar
Chiquita Harris
Eulalia Trahan Jones
Jennifer Dempster
Cherie Wilson
Charles Porter
Miles Crumley
Joanne Yancey
Weslia Echols
Maxine Peete
Tonya Guy
Michele Murner
Kathleen Simays
Chaunna Higgins
Janine Meriweather
Michelle Duquette

# APPENDIX

———

## Introduction

Office of Personnel Management. 2022. *Government-Wide DEIA: Our Progress and Path Forward to Building a Better Workforce for the American People.* https://www.opm.gov/policy-data-oversight/diversity-equity-inclusion-and-accessibility/reports/DEIA-Annual-Report-2022.pdf.

Riccucci, Norma M. 2021. *Managing Diversity in Public Sector Workforces,* 2nd edition. New York, NY: Routledge.

Saxon, Nicholas, Paul Villena, Sean Wilburn, Sarah Andersen, Dylan Maloney, and Ross Jacobson. 2023. *Census of Governments, Survey of Public Employment & Payroll Summary Report.* Washington, DC: US Department of Commerce.

US Equal Employment Opportunity Commission. 2020. *FY 2020 Annual Report on the Federal Workforce Part 2: Workforce Statistics and EEO Commitment.* Washington, DC: US Equal Employment Opportunity Commission. https://www.eeoc.gov/fy-2020-annual-report-federal-workforce-part-2-workforce-statistics-and-eeo-commitment.

US Equal Employment Opportunity Commission. 2021. "Job Patterns for Minorities and Women in State and Local Government (EEO-4)." Washington, DC: US Equal Employment Opportunity Commission. https://www.eeoc.gov/data/job-patterns-minorities-and-women-state-and-local-government-eeo-4.

## Chapter 1

Mengers, Abigail A. 2014. "The Benefits of Being Yourself: An Examination of Authenticity, Uniqueness, and Well-Being." Master of Applied Positive Psychology (MAPP) Capstone Projects. University of Pennsylvania.

Seligman, M. E. P. 2002. "Positive Psychology, Positive Prevention, and Positive Therapy." In *Handbook of Positive Psychology*, edited by C. R. Snyder and S. J. Lopez, 3-9. Oxford: Oxford University Press.

## Chapter 2

Heath, Kathryn, Jill Flynn, and Mary Davis Holt. 2014. *Women, Find Your Voice*. Brighton, MA: Harvard.

Tannen, Deborah. 1995. *The Power of Talk: Who Gets Heard and Why*. Brighton, MA: Harvard.

Thomas, Rachel, Marianne Cooper, Kate Urban, et al., 2021. *Women in the Workplace 2021*. New York, NY: McKinsey and Lean In. https://www.mckinsey.com/~/media/mckinsey/featured%20insights/diversity%20and%20inclusion/women%20in%20the%20workplace%202021/women-in-the-workplace-2021.pdf.

## Chapter 3

Goebig, Micha. 2022. "Three Beliefs about Confidence That Might Be Holding You Back as a Woman in Business." *Leadership* (blog), *Forbes*. March 8, 2022. https://www.forbes.com/sites/forbescoachescouncil/2022/03/08/three-beliefs-about-confidence-that-might-be-holding-you-back-as-a-woman-in-business/.

Powell, Katherine C. 2009. "The Role of Concept of Self and Societal Expectations in Academic and Career Achievement." *Journal of Adult Education* 38, no. 2: 32-40.

## Chapter 4

Munro, Ian. 2022. "A Roadmap for Career Development: How to Set Your Course." *Professional Development* (blog), *BetterUp*. May 31, 2022. https://www.betterup.com/blog/career-development.

Stringer, Kate, Jennifer Kerpelman, and Vladimir Skorikov. 2011. "Career Preparation: A Longitudinal, Process-Oriented Examination." *Journal of Vocational Behavior* 79, no. 1 (August): 158-169. doi:10.1016/j.jvb.2010.12.012.

Women in Fire (@Women in Fire). 2023. "Meet Our New President—Toni Washington." LinkedIn, February 2023. https://www.linkedin.com/posts/women-in-fire_blackhistorymonth-womeninfire-activity-7027697408792793089-ImHW/.

Women of Fire. 2023. "Women of Fire." *Our Stories* (blog), African American Fire Fighter Museum. Accessed August 28, 2023. https://www.aaffmuseum.org/our-stories/arnett-hartsfield-2/.

## Chapter 5

Mishra, Paresh, and Kimberly McDonald. 2017. "Career Resilience: An Integrated Review of the Empirical Literature." *Human Resource Development Review 16*, no. 3 (July): 1-30. doi:10.1177/1534484317719622.

Riggio, Ronald E. 2016. "Why Your Friends May Know You Better Than You Do." *Friends* (blog), *Psychology Today*. June 26, 2016. https://www.psychologytoday.com/intl/blog/cutting-edge-leadership/201606/why-your-friends-may-know-you-better-you-do.

Sargent, Jan. 2023. "The Resilience Mindset: Cultivating Inner Strength for Life's Ups and Downs." *Fit Mind Happy Heart Coaching* (blog). May 26, 2023. https://fitmindhappyheartcoaching.com/2023/05/26/building-resilience-and-inner-strength-with-hypnotherapy-and-coaching/.

## Chapter 6

Craig-Henderson, Kellina. 2020. "I've Been There. Fighting Stereotypes in the World of Science." *Science Matters* (blog), National Science Foundation. December 8, 2020. https://new.nsf.gov/science-matters/ive-been-there-fighting-stereotypes-world-science.

Eberhardt, Jennifer L., and Linda Tropp. 2021. "The Contact Conundrum: Reducing Conflict through Intergroup Contact." *Observer* (blog), *Psychological Science*. September/October 2021. https://www.psychologicalscience.org/observer/contact-conundrum.

Harris-Perry, Melissa V. 2011. *Sister Citizen Shame, Stereotypes, and Black Women in America*. New Haven, CT: Yale University Press.

Health and Human Services. n.d. *Combating Implicit Bias and Stereotypes*. Accessed September 5, 2023. https://thinkculturalhealth.hhs.gov/assets/pdfs/resource-library/combating-implicit-bias-stereotypes.pdf.

Jones, Charisse, and Kumea Shorter-Gooden. 2004. *Shifting: The Double Lives of Black Women in America*. New York, NY: Perennial.

Lloyd, Camille. 2021. "One in Four Black Workers Report Discrimination at Work." *News* (blog), *Gallup*. January 12, 2021. https://news.gallup.com/poll/328394/one-four-black-workers-report-discrimination-work.aspx.

Martens, Andy, Michael Johns, Jeff Greenberg, and Jeff Schimel. 2006. "Combating Stereotype Threat: The Effect of Self-affirmation on Women's Intellectual Performance." *Journal of Experimental Social Psychology* 42, no. 2 (March): 236-243. https://doi.org/10.1016/j.jesp.2005.04.010.

Smith, Ella Bell, and Stella M. Nkomo. 2021. *Our Separate Ways: Black and White Women and the Struggle for Professional Identity*. Boston, MA: Harvard Business Review Press.

Wong, Chuk Yan E., Teri A. Kirby, Floor Rink, and Michelle K. Ryan. 2022. "Intersectional Invisibility in Women's Diversity Interventions." *Frontiers in Psychology* 13 (May). https://doi.org/10.3389/fpsyg.2022.791572.

## Chapter 7

Nawaz, Amna, Candice Norwood, and Matt Loffman. 2021. "For Black Women in Government, Highlighting Threats and Abuse Can Make It Worse." *PBS News Hour.* June 29, 2021.

https://www.pbs.org/newshour/show/for-black-women-in-government-highlighting-threats-and-abuse-can-make-it-worse.

Norwood, Candice, Chloe Jones, and Lizz Bolaji. 2021. "More Black Women Are Being Elected to Office. Few Feel Safe Once They Get There." *Politics* (blog), PBS. June 17, 2021. https://www.pbs.org/newshour/politics/more-black-women-are-being-elected-to-office-few-feel-safe-once-they-get-there.

Schaeffer, Katherine. 2023. "22 States Have Ever Elected a Black Woman to Congress." *Short Reads* (blog), Pew Research Center. February 16, 2023. https://www.pewresearch.org/short-reads/2023/02/16/22-states-have-ever-elected-a-black-woman-to-congress/.

Shardhana, Dhanraj. 2023. "The Impact of a Hostile Working Environment on Work-Life Balance." Thesis. National College of Ireland. https://norma.ncirl.ie/6793/1/dhanrajshardhana.pdf.

## Chapter 8

American Psychological Association. 2019. "Perseverance toward Life Goals Can Fend Off Depression, Anxiety, Panic Disorders." Accessed September 23, 2023. https://www.apa.org/news/press/releases/2019/05/goals-perseverance.

Bergland, Christopher. 2011. "The Neuroscience of Perseverance." *The Athlete's Way* (blog), *Psychology Today*. December 26, 2011. https://www.psychologytoday.com/us/blog/the-athletes-way/201112/the-neuroscience-perseverance.

Bergland, Christopher. 2019. "Perseverance Cultivate Purposefulness and Boosts Resilience." *The Athlete's Way* (blog), *Psychology Today*. May 4, 2019. https://www.psychologytoday.com/us/blog/the-athletes-way/201905/perseverance-cultivates-purposefulness-and-boosts-resilience.

Shaffner, Anna Katharina. 2020. "Perseverance in Psychology: Meaning, Importance & Books." *Strengths & Virtues* (blog), *Positive Psychology.* September 16, 2020. https://positivepsychology.com/perseverance/.

## Chapter 9

Clark, Dorie. 2018. "How Women Can Develop—and Promote—Their Personal Brand." *Personal Brand* (blog), *Harvard Business Review.* March 2, 2018. https://hbr.org/2018/03/how-women-can-develop-and-promote-their-personal-brand.

Peters, Tom. 1997. "The Brand Called You." *Fast Company*, August/September 1997. https://www.fastcompany.com/28905/brand-called-you.

Petra, Zidar, and Miha Maric. 2015. "Personal Brand." Paper presented at the 34th International Conference on Organizational Science Development, Portorož, Slovenia, March 2015. https://www.researchgate.net/publication/274073688_Personal_brand.

Starheim, Rianna P. 2019. *Women in Policing: Breaking Barriers and Blazing a Path.* Washington, DC: US Department of Justice.

Wensil, B., and W. Ernst. 2023. "How Successful Women Sustain Career Momentum." *Diversity and Inclusion* (blog), *Harvard Business Review.* January 16, 2023. https://hbr.org/2023/01/how-successful-women-sustain-career-momentum.

## Chapter 10

Kay, Katty, and Claire Shipman. 2014. "The Confidence Gap." *The Atlantic,* May 2014.

https://www.theatlantic.com/magazine/archive/2014/05/the-confidence-gap/359815/.

Lewis, Greg. 2020. "LinkedIn Data Shows Women Are Less Likely to Have Strong Networks—Here's What Companies Should Do." *Talent* (blog), LinkedIn. March 11, 2020. https://www.linkedin.com/business/talent/blog/talent-acquisition/women-less-likely-to-have-strong-networks.

Roberts, Laura Morgan, and Anthony J. Mayo. 2020. "Remote Networking as a Person of Color." *Professional Networks* (blog), *Harvard Business Review*. September 7, 2020. https://hbr.org/2020/09/remote-networking-as-a-person-of-color.

## Chapter 11

Chow, Rosalind. 2021. "Don't Just Mentor Women and People of Color. Sponsor Them." *Diversity and Inclusion* (blog), *Harvard Business Review*. June 30, 2021. https://hbr.org/2021/06/dont-just-mentor-women-and-people-of-color-sponsor-them.

Ekpe, Leslie, and Sarah Toutant. 2022. "Moving beyond Performative Allyship: A Conceptual Framework for Anti-racist Co-conspirators." In *Developing Anti-Racist Practices in the Helping Professions: Inclusive Theory, Pedagogy, and Application,* edited by K. F. Johnson, N. M. Sparkman-Key, A. Meca and S. Z. Tarver, 67-91. Cham: Palgrave Macmillan.

Elligrud, Kweilin, Alexis Krivkovich, Marie-Claude Nadeau, and Jill Zucker. 2021. "Closing the Gender and Race Gaps in North American Financial Services." *Financial Services* (blog), McKinsey. October 21, 2021. https://www.mckinsey.com/industries/financial-services/our-insights/closing-the-gender-and-race-gaps-in-north-american-financial-services.

Mcilongo, M., and K. Strydom. 2021. "The Significance of Mentorship in Supporting the Career Advancement of Women in the Public Sector." *Heliyon* 7, no. 6 (June): 1-9. https://doi.org/10.1016/j.heliyon.2021.e07321.

Omadeke, Janice. 2021. "What's the Difference between a Mentor and a Sponsor?" *Career Planning* (blog), *Harvard Business Review.* October 20, 2021. https://hbr.org/2021/10/whats-the-difference-between-a-mentor-and-a-sponsor.

Patel, Hena. 2017. "Forget a Mentor Find a Sponsor." Review of *Forget a Mentor Find a Sponsor* by Sylvia Ann Hewlett. https://www.acc.org/Membership/Sections-and-Councils/Women-in-Cardiology-Section/Section-Updates/2017/07/26/15/32/Book-Review-Forget-a-Mentor-Find-a-Sponsor.

Smith, Ella Bell, and Stella M. Nkomo. 2021. *Our Separate Ways: Black and White Women and the Struggle for Professional Identity.* Boston, MA: Harvard Business Review Press.

## Conclusion

Office of Personnel Management. 2022. *Government-Wide DEIA: Our Progress and Path Forward to Building a Better Workforce for the American People.* Washington, DC: Office of Personnel Management. https://www.opm.gov/policy-data-oversight/diversity-equity-inclusion-and-accessibility/reports/DEIA-Annual-Report-2022.pdf.

US Equal Employment Opportunity Commission. 2021. *Job Patterns for Minorities and Women in State and Local Government (EEO-4).* Washington, DC: US Equal Employment Opportunity Commission. https://www.eeoc.gov/data/job-patterns-minorities-and-women-state-and-local-government-eeo-4.

Made in the USA
Middletown, DE
13 September 2024

60916873R00106